Canadian
Dinosaurs

Canadian Dinosaurs

ELIN KELSEY

MAPLE
TREE
PRESS

Maple Tree Press Inc.
51 Front Street East, Suite 200
Toronto, Ontario M5E 1B3
www.mapletreepress.com

Distributed in Canada by Raincoast Books
9050 Shaughnessy Street
Vancouver, British Columbia V6P 6E5

Distributed in the United States by
Publishers Group West
1700 Fourth Street
Berkeley, California 94710

We acknowledge the financial support of the
Canada Council for the Arts, the Ontario Arts
Council, the Government of Canada through
the Book Publishing Industry Development
Program (BPIDP), and the Government of
Ontario through the Ontario Media
Development Corporation's Book Initiative
for our publishing activities.

Cataloguing in Publication Data
Kelsey, Elin
          Canadian dinosaurs / Elin Kelsey. —
Updated ed.

(A Wow Canada! book)
Includes index.
ISBN 13: 978-1-897349-08-3 (bound)
ISBN 10: 1-897349-08-4 (bound)
ISBN 13: 978-1-897066-85-0 (pbk.)
ISBN 10: 1-897066-85-6 (pbk.)

1. Dinosaurs—Canada—Juvenile literature.
2. Paleontology—Juvenile literature.
I. Title. II. Series: Wow Canada! book

QE861.5.K44 2007   j567.90971
C2007-901780-0

Acknowledgements
This book could never have been written
without the generosity and good humour of
palaeontologists and other lovers of
prehistoric life. Warm thanks to the
following individuals for their stories, ideas,
and enthusiasms: Dennis Braman, Don
Brinkman, Karen Chin, Stephen Cumbaa,
Philip Currie, Richard Day, Rob Holmes, Paul
Johnston, Eva Koppelhus, Rich McCrea,
Michael Ryan, Donna Sloan, Wendy Sloboda,
Eric Snively, John Storer, Hans-Dieter Sues,
Darren Tanke, Tim Tokaryk, and Darla
Zelenitsky. Special thanks to Sheba Meland
for dreaming up this fabulous book and
inviting me to write it, and to Anne Shone,
Kat Mototsune, Victoria Hill, and Word &
Image Design Studio for transforming the
material into the lovely pages that you are
about to explore. Big hugs to Matthias Neill
and Jason Hoech for their demonstrations of
the passion that dinosaurs can inspire in
young hearts, and to Andy Johnson for
everything.

Dedication
For Matthias, Lucas, Karen, and Kip—
intrepid members of the Canadian dinosaur
expedition, winter 2001

Scientific review:
Stephen Cumbaa and Richard Day

Design & art direction:
Word & Image Design Studio
(www.wordandimagedesign.com)

Front cover illustration:
Gorgosaurus libratus by Christopher Srnka

Printed in China

B C D E F

CONTENTS

THE EXCITING WORLD OF DINOSAUR DISCOVERY

How many dinosaurs can you name? If you're a keen dinosaur enthusiast, you may be able to dazzle your friends with a list of twenty or more multi-syllabic mouthfuls. So far, 500 species of dinosaurs have been discovered worldwide, but palaeontologists (scientists who study ancient life) are convinced that thousands and thousands of new kinds of dinosaurs will be identified in the years to come. So, if you become a dinosaur scientist, there's a very good chance that you could one day discover a new dinosaur species.

Dinosaurs were not the big, slow, stupid animals we once thought they were. It's clear that they were a surprisingly diverse group. Some were as tiny as the birds you see on a city street; others were large enough to balance on a see-saw with a blue whale. They lived in jungles, in ice fields, or in bone-dry deserts; some may have hibernated or migrated. And there is growing evidence that many dinosaurs lived in large social groups, and that young dinosaurs relied on their parents' care for the first months, and maybe even years, of their lives.

Dinosaurs were as fascinating and different from one another as you are from a chipmunk or a walrus. New species of dinosaurs evolved and others disappeared many, many times during the 160 million years that we now call the age of dinosaurs. In fact, dinosaurs were on Earth at least *forty times* as long as humans have been here!

As you read this book, you'll see that ideas about dinosaurs are always changing and that palaeontologists often disagree about how certain dinosaurs lived. This makes sense when you consider that no one has ever seen a living dinosaur. Everything we think we know about dinosaurs is interpreted from the fossilized remains of their dead bodies or from trace fossils, fossils formed when a dinosaur was still alive, such as footprints, trackways, eggs, nests, or "poops."

Each new discovery provides a palaeontologist with a chance to question assumptions, even those upon which their own work is based. New technologies let them test new theories or look at familiar fossils in new ways. Look for the special profiles of researchers, dinosaurs, and trace-fossil finds scattered throughout this book to alert you to some "hot-off-the-press" dinosaur debates.

CANADA IS DINOSAUR COUNTRY

▲

Would you like to step back in time and walk among full-sized dinosaur models in natural environments? Then the Calgary Zoo's Prehistoric Park is the place for you.

Maple leaves, Mounties, and…*Tyrannosaurus rex*! Canada is world-famous for its rich dinosaur heritage. Whether you're tiptoeing through a prairie field in Saskatchewan, or hiking along an ocean cliff in Nova Scotia, there may be a dinosaur bone buried deep beneath your feet.

Every year, millions of people travel through Canada to marvel at the impressive dinosaur skeletons on display at the Royal Ontario Museum in Toronto, the Canadian Museum of Nature in Ottawa, and the Royal Tyrrell Museum of Palaeontology in Alberta. Adventurous types can satisfy their dinosaur desires with trips to the T. rex Discovery Centre in Eastend, Saskatchewan, the Devil's Coulee Dinosaur Heritage Museum in Alberta's badlands, or the Fundy Geological Museum in Nova Scotia. Look on page 92 for a list of dinosaur destinations.

Imagine the thrill of scaling a cliffside chock-a-block full of dinosaur footprints, or unearthing the secret clues that suggest that enormous sauropods were once Canadian residents. Within the pages of this book, you'll find the latest scoop on great Canadian dinosaur finds, and the intriguing people that make Canada a world leader in dinosaur discovery.

▲

Whether you prefer to dig dinosaurs in Alberta's Dinosaur Provincial Park, like these kids, or watch scientists prepare fossils in their labs, there is a Canadian dinosaur expedition to suit all of your dinosaur cravings.

▼

WHY CANADA?

▲
Day dawns, about 75 million years ago (mya), in the area that is now Dinosaur Provincial Park in Alberta. Groups of duckbill and horned dinosaurs in the waters of a bayou; a small carnivore pauses beneath a magnolia; ostrich dinosaurs approach the water's edge to drink; a soft-shelled turtle suns itself.

Why is Canada such a fabulous place for dinosaurs? World-famous Canadian palaeontologist Philip Currie (see Profile on page 39) says that it's a unique combination of factors.

For one thing, many of the prehistoric environments that existed in Canada during the Mesozoic Era, 230–65 million years ago (mya) were great places for dinosaurs to live. Seventy-five million years ago, for instance, the landmass where Alberta is now located was in a different location. The duckbill and horned dinosaurs living then preferred its cool but still mild climate (see page 12). Many scientists believe that these large plant-eaters migrated from the

Arctic to southern Alberta each year. This might explain why so many duckbill and horned dinosaur skeletons are found there.

When dinosaurs died, the many rivers, lakes, and even inland seas of Canada's prehistoric environments created ideal conditions for quick burial and eventual fossilization. So, not only was Canada a great place for dinosaurs to live, it was also a good place for them to die.

And, last but not least, the glaciers that carved away tons and tons of more recent rock, and the badland rivers and winds that continue to do so, make it possible to get at the rock layers that contain dinosaur fossils.

A great place to live, a great place to die, and a great place to be found: That's what makes Canada such a great place for dinosaurs.

DINOSAUR PROVINCIAL PARK

Where's the best place in the world to find large, mostly-complete dinosaur skeletons? Alberta's Dinosaur Provincial Park. In some parts of the park there are so many fossils, it's difficult to walk without stepping on tiny bits of dinosaur bones and teeth.

This area's well-preserved fossil environments have been attracting scientists from all over the world since before your grandparents were born. With so many years of research to draw upon, scientists can be relatively certain of the age of the fossils they find. This allows them to study how certain groups of dinosaurs changed over time and what animals shared the same prehistoric habitats. Thanks to the nearby Royal Tyrrell Museum of Palaeontology, scientists can also compare the fossils they discover to those previously collected from the park and stored in the museum's amazing collections area.

▲
What a difference time makes! Today, Dinosaur Provincial Park is dry, with lots of exposed rock— perfect conditions for fossil hunting, like the excavation of this *Albertosaurus* bone bed.

DINOSAUR COUNTRY THEN

A dinosaur's paradise of huge trees and ferns, Cathedral Forest on Vancouver Island is what scientists think Cretaceous environments might have been like. For clues to the world dinosaurs lived in, scientists look to palaeobotany, the study of ancient plants.

When duckbill and horned dinosaurs lived in Canada, the vast area of forests and lakes extended north to what is Arctic tundra today. Large groups of dinosaurs likely ate their way through the dense forests on their northward migration each spring, and returned southward as the sunlight dwindled each fall.

Knowledge of prehistoric plants and environments is changing. When the Royal Tyrrell Museum opened its palaeoconservatory (a living exhibit of plants from more than 65 million years ago) in 1985, nearly all the plants were tropical. Today, you might need a sweater for a walk through. More recent evidence suggests that Alberta had a cooler climate 80–65 million years ago.

Growth rings in fossilized trees (such as this conifer from Alberta) and in some dinosaur bones tell palaeontologists the Canada of 75 million years ago had true seasons. But the seasons were determined by wet and dry cycles, not cold or warm weather.

Leaves are the next most common plant fossil after wood. Only hardy leaves were likely to survive the process of fossilization—these ones above were alive 65 million years ago.

Scientists don't have a really good idea of the plants that dinosaurs ate. Most of what they do know about the diet of plant-eating dinosaurs is from pollen grains in rare pieces of dinosaur "poop" or from bits of wood found in dinosaur stomach cavities. Unfortunately, they can't always tell if the wood was eaten by the dinosaur or if it ended up in the carcass once the body started to decay.

Dennis Braman is particularly interested in pollen and spores—the reproductive parts of plants. Hardier than fossilized leaves, great examples are found throughout Alberta, Saskatchewan, Manitoba, and the west coast of Vancouver Island. The challenge is that pollen and spores are designed to be spread by wind and water, so finding a fossilized pollen grain in one place doesn't mean that the plant actually grew there. Dennis is currently studying five pollen specimens that came from widely scattered locations in Colorado, Alberta, Saskatchewan, and Alaska. A far as pollen grains go, they are great big clunkers that are too heavy to have been carried a long way by wind. Dennis suspects they were carried by birds—a strong clue that some Cretaceous birds might have been migratory.

Researcher Profile: Dennis Braman

Dennis was always interested in biology, but high-school teachers advised him against it, so he decided to major in geology at university. In his final year of undergraduate studies, he took a course in palynology (the study of fossil spores and pollen), and discovered that it was possible to link his love of living organisms with his love of fossils. Today, he is Curator of Palynology at the Royal Tyrrell Museum of Palaeontology.

DINOSAUR COUNTRY NOW

▲

Compare the Alberta badlands (big picture) to this city scene in New Jersey, U.S.A. Both sites contain dinosaur fossils, but in New Jersey they are buried under the cement and skyscrapers. Luckily for dinosaur hunters, the cold, harsh winters, sparse vegetation, and seasonal floods of the badlands have kept many areas from being developed by people.

Is there a dinosaur in your backyard? Drive a shovel into a garden and imagine unearthing a dinosaur lying deep within the rocks under the soil. It's a thrilling idea, but how likely is it to happen? Depending upon where you live in Canada, it may be more possible than you think. Dinosaurs were so plentiful in what is now the city of Edmonton, Alberta, that nine bone beds, each containing the fossil remains of several duckbill dinosaurs, have been found within the city limits. And, if you live in Grande Prairie, Alberta, you can count a recent discovery of hundreds of horned dinosaurs as fellow city residents.

Ontario was probably a good place to find dinosaurs, at least before the massive glaciers of the ice ages scraped off sedimentary rock layers down to the Canadian Shield. Any dinosaurs buried in those sediments are likely to have been transported to somebody's backyard in Ohio or Michigan!

South of the Canadian border in Connecticut, New Jersey, and Virginia, there are many Triassic- and Jurassic-aged rock formations that could contain dinosaurs. Trouble is, they're overgrown by forests or buried beneath cities.

LOOKING FOR DINOSAURS USUALLY BEGINS WITH LOOKING AT ROCKS

Dinosaurs are found in rocks formed in the Mesozoic Era (about 230–65 mya). Palaeontologists start with detailed maps showing different types of rock, looking for ones that might contain specific kinds of dinosaur fossils. Since different dinosaurs lived at different times, palaeontologists often work closely with geologists (scientists who study rocks) to get accurate estimates of the age of rock formations. Next, they narrow the search by looking at environments likely to have preserved dinosaur remains, such as a rock deposit by a river. Finally, they go to areas where rocks of the right age and the right environment are well exposed—it's almost impossible to find dinosaur fossils beneath, say, a maple forest or a mall parking lot.

How old are the rocks in your neighbourhood? Check out the Geological Survey of Canada website (http://gsc.nrcan.gc.ca) for a map that will show you.

The rock layers that contain dinosaur fossils are youngsters compared to the Canadian Shield. This granddaddy of rock layers is 3.6–1.8 billion years old, and extends over eastern, central, and northwestern Canada from the Great Lakes to the Canadian Arctic.

▼

DINOSAUR HUNTING

Mark Turner (left) and Daniel Helm (right) with the dinosaur footprints they found. Baby powder was sprinkled on the footprints so they would show up better in the photograph.

You may not be able to take a step in some parts of Alberta without treading on a dinosaur part, but head a little farther west to British Columbia, and finding a dinosaur is very rare indeed. Until 2001, only one dinosaur bone had ever been found in the entire province. Daniel Helm (aged nine) and Mark Turner (aged eleven) had no idea they were about to add three to that number, and double the number of dinosaurs found in their home province.

That August, the boys were tubing down rapids at Flatbed Creek in Tumbler Ridge. Mark fell out of his tube, so the boys headed to shore, where they discovered impressions on the ground. They looked at each other and said, "Dinosaur tracks!"

The boys went home and called a local palaeontologist, who suggested they call Rich McCrea (see Profile on page 68). Rich travelled to the site and confirmed that the footprints were made by an ankylosaur (armoured dinosaur).

The luck didn't stop there. When Rich began the thorough process of surveying and measuring the track, he set his compass down, and…surprise! The compass had come to rest on a dinosaur bone. By the end of 2006, more than 200 bones had been found and excavated from the canyon, making it British Columbia's first (and western Canada's oldest) accumulation of dinosaur skeletal material, including ankylosaur and nodosaur (armoured dinosaurs) and hadrosaurs (duckbill dinosaurs).

▶ Mark and Daniel stand by their trackway find with Rich McCrea.

▲ Did an ankylosaur like this one roam in what is now British Columbia? Thanks to two boys, we know the answer is "yes!"

Researcher Profile: J.B. Tyrrell

Joseph Burr Tyrrell spent most of his long career as a geologist, explorer, and entrepreneur on the Canadian Shield. Yet it was his discovery of an *Albertosaurus* skull for which he is most famous. Joseph was working for the Geological Survey of Canada, mapping the distribution of coal along the new southern route of the Canadian Pacific Railway, when he found the skull near what is today Drumheller, Alberta. The Royal Tyrrell Museum of Palaeontology, one of the most famous palaeontological museums in the world, was named in his honour.

DIGGING IT

▲

George Sternberg, one of the famous family of dinosaur hunters from early in the 20th century, at an excavation in Steveville, Alberta, in 1921.

What did people think dinosaur bones were before anyone knew there were such things as dinosaurs? "The grandfather of the buffalo" is how the Piegan, an aboriginal people of Alberta, described dinosaur bones to Jean-Baptiste L'Heureux, a French-Canadian who travelled to the badlands in the mid-1800s. Two hundred years earlier, an Englishman named Robert Plot published the first written account of a dinosaur bone in his book *The Natural History of Oxfordshire*. Although Plot recognized that the fossil was "a real bone, now petrified," he assumed from its size that it must be "the Bone of some Elephant."

Fossilized footprints have inspired their own special legends. Dinosaur tracks in the Connecticut Valley were thought to be those of a raven that failed to return to Noah's Ark. Dragons were held responsible for making the tracks found in the Rhine Valley of Germany. A dinosaur footprint built into the porch wall of a church in Cheshire, England, was believed to be the devil's toenail!

The first time the word "dinosaur" was used was in 1842, when Richard Owen, a British palaeontologist, applied it to three impressively large fossil reptiles from the English countryside: *Megalosaurus*, *Iguanodon*, and *Hylaeosaurus*. Few new dinosaurs would be discovered in Britain for the next 130 years but, thanks to Richard Owen, Britain will always hold the special privilege of being the birthplace of the dinosaurs.

The science of studying dinosaur fossils began in earnest in 1858 with the discovery of the first nearly complete dinosaur skeleton in Haddonfield, New Jersey. Although individual bones had been found and studied earlier in both Europe and North America, this was the find that included enough bones of the same animal to scientifically prove dinosaurs had really existed. The dinosaur, named *Hadrosaurus foulkii,* was the first dinosaur skeleton ever mounted and displayed in public.

Before the discovery of the first nearly complete dinosaur skeleton, *Hadrosaurus foulkii*, scientists had no way of "looking" at a dinosaur. With only individual bones or parts of a skeleton to work from, they assumed that dinosaurs walked on four legs like most large mammals do today. Because it was possible to see that the hind legs of *Hadrosaurus foulkii* were much bigger than its forelimbs, this skeleton provided the first hint that some dinosaurs might have walked on two legs instead of on all fours.

▼

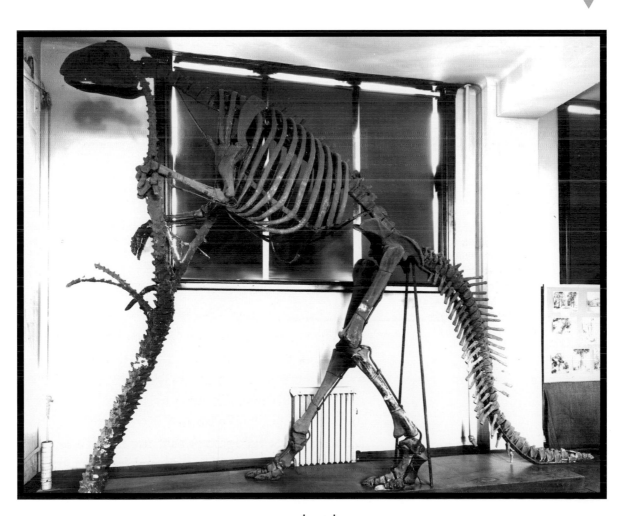

THE GREAT CANADIAN DINOSAUR RUSH

▲

Roughing it at C.M. Sternberg's first camp near the mouth of Sand Creek, Alberta, in 1917. Digging for dinosaurs in the badlands was hard work: long, hot, bug-filled days in summer; bitterly cold, windy days in winter.

The swashbuckling story of looking for dinosaurs in Canada began long ago, when your great-great-grandparents were kids. We now know that Alberta's Red Deer River valley is rich in dinosaur fossils. Imagine how exciting it would have been to have first discovered this—as Joseph Tyrrell (see Profile on page 17) did when he found the skull of an *Albertosaurus*, a smaller relative of *T. rex*.

In the early 1900s, fossil hunters working for major museums around the world rushed to Alberta to collect dinosaur skeletons for display. The Geological Survey of Canada (GSC) didn't want to see all the best Canadian dinosaur finds exported to other countries. So they sent a collector named

Charles Sternberg, along with his sons, to Alberta for dinosaurs worthy of display at the National Museum of Canada (now the Canadian Museum of Nature) in Ottawa.

At the same time, Barnum Brown (the famous American dinosaur hunter who first discovered *Tyrannosaurus rex*) combed the area in search of dinosaurs for the American Museum of Natural History in New York. The competition for dinosaurs was so intense, it sparked a period in history dubbed the Great Canadian Dinosaur Rush.

THE GREAT DINOSAUR REVOLUTION

Dinosaur research nearly came to a stop during the Great Depression of the 1930s and World War II in the 1940s. During the 1950s, scientists focused on fossil mammals from the ice ages.

But by the 1970s, palaeontologists began to think of dinosaurs not just as spectacular museum specimens, but as animals that could be studied the same as any other animal group. Investigations of nesting sites, migration routes, dinosaur herds, and trackways—a new style of dinosaur research—began. Thanks to these fresh approaches, we've gained more knowledge about dinosaurs in the past 30 years than in the 160 years since dinosaurs were first discovered.

◄ Barnum Brown's parents named their son after the famous circus showman P.T. Barnum, to spruce up his ordinary surname, and he went on to live up to it. Brown enjoyed a spectacularly successful 66-year career in palaeontology.

Researcher Profile: Alice E. Wilson

Alice E. Wilson was the first female geologist hired by the Geological Survey of Canada. Alice joined the Survey as a museum assistant, performing mainly clerical duties. But by 1913 she had begun her career in palaeontology with a paper published in the first of the Museum bulletins. Alice became one of Canada's leading scientists.

THE DINOSAUR DREAM TEAM

▲

The Sternbergs were among the world's most successful dinosaur hunters. This picture shows George Sternberg packing a dinosaur for removal to the University of Alberta.

You probably know families of teachers or farmers or computer programmers, but have you ever heard of a family of dinosaur hunters? Charles H. Sternberg, along with his sons, George, Charlie (Charles M.), and Levi, had a fossil-hunting business that lasted from 1906 to 1916. They were so amazingly good at finding high-quality dinosaur specimens—and lots of them—that historians call them the "dinosaur dream team." From 1912 to 1916, when the Sternbergs worked in Alberta, they collected 20 dinosaur skeletons and thousands of other fossil specimens. Among these were an *Albertosaurus*, several horned dinosaurs, and many duckbill dinosaur specimens.

The Sternbergs were innovators in the development of new ways to collect fossils. More than 125 years ago, Charles H. pioneered the technique of "jacketing" bones in a protective case of burlap and plaster that is still used today. Years later, his youngest son, Levi, perfected a latex casting technique that scientists and technicians continue to use to duplicate fossils.

DINOSAURS FOR THE WORLD

Charlie Sternberg knew just how special Alberta's badlands were for dinosaur fossils. Long past the age when most people retire, he worked with the provincial government to establish Dinosaur Provincial Park. Today, it is a UNESCO World Heritage Site—recognized by the United Nations for its unique natural environments and its extraordinary fossil wealth.

Researcher Profile: The Sternbergs

Charles H. Sternberg (1850–1943)

Charles H. began hunting fossils as a boy near his family's home in upstate New York, and he spent the next 70 years pursuing his dinosaur passion. He collected tens of thousands of specimens, including the first identifiable specimen of *Triceratops*. He was a dreamer who always believed an even greater fossil was yet to be found.

George F. Sternberg (1883–1969)

While visiting his father's field camp, nine-year-old George wandered away and discovered a nearly complete plesiosaur skeleton! He collected many important specimens during his career, including a duckbill dinosaur (*Edmontosaurus regalis*) with fossilized muscle and skin—the first remains of flesh found on a dinosaur skeleton.

Charles M. "Charlie" Sternberg (1885–1981)

Fourteen-year-old Charlie excavated fossils with his father and older brother while on breaks from school. After the family's fossil-hunting business ended in 1916, he continued to collect dinosaurs for the Geological Survey of Canada well into his 80s. Charlie made many important finds, including the first specimen of the duckbill dinosaur *Brachylophosaurus canadensis*.

Levi Sternberg (1894–1976)

Like his brothers, Levi worked for his dad before joining the Royal Ontario Museum, where he spent most of his career. A good-humoured fellow, he liked the hot, strenuous, and often tedious work of excavating specimens, leaving others to prepare them in the lab. His many accomplishments include the discovery of the first specimen of the horned dinosaur *Chasmosaurus brevirostris*.

DEEP-SEA PALAEONTOLOGY

The maiden voyage of the *SS Mount Temple* (seen above) was September 19, 1901. On the night of April 14, 1912, only 78 km (49 miles) away when *RMS Titanic* struck an iceberg and sank, *Mount Temple* was one of the closest ships to the tragedy, but ice blocked her way and she could not assist.

By 1916, both the National Museum of Canada and the American Museum of Natural History had decided to stop sending dinosaur hunters to Alberta. But Charles Sternberg was eager to continue collecting in dinosaur-rich Alberta. He convinced the British Museum of Natural History to hire him to send dinosaurs to them in London, England. Sternberg's first shipment of dinosaurs crossed the Atlantic safely. The second was not so lucky.

The *SS Mount Temple*, a ship owned and operated by the Canadian Pacific Steamship Company, left Montreal in November 1916, bound for London. Within her fully loaded cargo, she carried twenty or so wooden crates from Charles Sternberg, containing the jacketed bones from three hadrosaurs, or duckbill dinosaurs—some with large patches of skin impressions! World War I was underway, so the *SS Mount Temple* was armed with a single deck gun for protection.

Ten days out to sea, a German surface raider attacked the *SS Mount Temple*. During the very short battle, 111 crew and passengers, as well as the crew's pet monkeys, cats, and canaries, were taken from the ship. Moments later…*BANG*! Explosive time charges ignited, the *Mount Temple* keeled over, and ship and cargo sank to the bottom of the North Atlantic Ocean.

The sunken duckbill dinosaur skeletons have been soaking in salt water at depths of 4,572 metres (15,000 feet) for the past 90 years. Could the fossils survive? Palaeontologists are buzzing with opinions on the subject. Fresh bone material breaks down in seawater, but fossilized bone is more likely to be preserved. Yet no one knows what the effects of long-term exposure to near-freezing seawater, under tremendous pressure, has on field jackets or dinosaur bones hardened in the field with shellac.

Are the lost dinosaurs of the *SS Mount Temple* still lying on the bottom of the Atlantic, or have they turned to sludge? This tantalizing deep-sea mystery is attracting a lot of attention. It may not be long before palaeontologists are packing their diving gear for their most unusual dinosaur-collecting trip ever!

TRANSATLANTIC DINOSAURS

It took weeks for Sternberg's first shipment to cross the Atlantic Ocean. But a recent discovery in Portugal suggests that *Allosaurus fragilis*, a carnivorous dinosaur that lived 150 million years ago, could cross the ocean on its own. Many allosaur fossils have been found in North America, but the Portuguese finds are the first in Europe that can be positively identified as the same species.

All of the continents were close together when dinosaurs originated 225 million years ago. They started to drift apart soon after that, and by 150 million years ago, the Atlantic is thought to have been 200 to 300 km (125 to 185 miles) wide and far too deep for dinosaurs to cross. The new discovery shows that significant bridges of land must have remained even when the Atlantic Ocean was already quite wide.

DIVING FOR DINOSAURS

Dinosaur enthusiasts can turn up in the most unexpected places. Don't be surprised if the next time you hear about Darren Tanke (see Profile on page 31) he's in a submersible vehicle for deep-sea exploration (see picture at right). In his spare time, Darren studies the sinking of the *SS Mount Temple*. Can the dinosaurs be recovered? Amazingly well-preserved objects found by marine archaeologists studying shipwrecks encourage Darren. Coal, clothing, food in jars, string, leather, rubber, natural-bristle brushes, and even personal letters have all been recovered from the famous 1912 wreck of the *RMS Titanic*, 3,800 metres (12,460 feet) beneath the ocean surface.

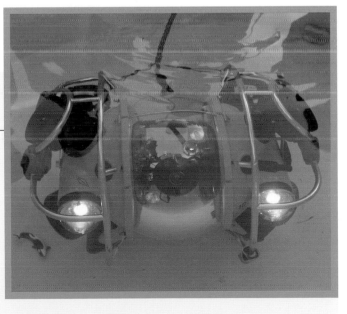

LOOKING BACK

The five o'clock edition of the Toronto *Evening Telegram* from Thursday, June 8, 1916. A scrap of this newspaper found in an old quarry, or dig, proved that it was here that Charles Sternberg found the dinosaur fossils that were lost when the *SS Mount Temple* was sunk.

A small scrap of newspaper discovered in Dinosaur Provincial Park in 2001 turned out to be a critical clue in identifying the quarry, or dig location, where the sunken dinosaurs of the *SS Mount Temple* originated.

Old dinosaur quarries are scattered across Dinosaur Provincial Park and beyond in Alberta. But how do you know when you're looking at one? Luckily, Nicolai Hernes and Tom Guldberg, two Norwegian students, had just attended a slide show given by Darren Tanke (see Profile on page 31) about lost and mystery quarries. The moment they discovered fragments of broken glass, a piece of wood from a crate, small pieces of plaster with embedded burlap fabric, and bits of old newspaper in the rugged badlands of Dinosaur Provincial Park, they knew they had found something important.

When Darren entered the quarry, he was reminded of some of Charles Sternberg's field-note descriptions and historical photographs. Was this the "lost" 1916 quarry, the source of the dinosaur bones that had sailed for England and been lost at the bottom of the sea? A scrap of newspaper turned out to be the best clue.

Early fossil hunters used newspapers for lining the plaster jackets, or for wrapping small bone pieces. Once buried, newspaper can last for decades. Because each edition of a newspaper is unique, even small fragments can help date a mystery quarry.

In this case, an advertisement mentioning Yonge Street immediately linked the paper to Toronto. But records showed that the Royal Ontario Museum (ROM) in Toronto did not work in Dinosaur Provincial Park until 1918. Levi Sternberg moved to Toronto in 1916, and it was possible that someone might have mailed the paper to him. Other advertisements listed places available for rent in summer months, a clue that the newspaper was a summer issue.

Armed with these clues, Kerri Kamra, a Toronto resident who had participated in the Tyrrell Museum's Field Experience program, volunteered to search back issues of newspapers stored on microfilm at the public library. She began with the year 1916 and, within two hours, she had tracked down a complete match—the 5 o'clock edition of *The Evening Telegram* (Toronto) from Thursday, June 8, 1916. The year and identity of the quarry were now confirmed. The original home of the sunken dinosaurs had been discovered!

LOST QUARRIES

Sometimes, the only clues that a quarry once existed are unidentified historical photographs taken decades earlier when the excavations were in progress. If you've ever seen old photographs of the neighbourhood where you live, you know how difficult it is to match an old photo to a modern location—trees grow, buildings are torn down or changed, and roads are built. Finding lost dinosaur quarries from historical photos is particularly tricky in the badlands, where erosion can dramatically change the shape of the landscape.

◄ Palaeontologists Philip Currie and Eva Koppelhus visited the mystery quarry for the first time in August 2001, and agreed that it matched this 1917 picture of Charles Sternberg's (arrow points to him) quarry 196.

THE TECHNOLOGY OF THE DIG

▲

A fossil preparation lab in the Canadian Museum of Nature's Research and Administration building. Note the hose-like vents dropping from the ceiling; these are used to suck up the dust while the technicians use the tiny drills and chisels to remove the fossils from their plaster jackets. Coiled electrical cord dispensers also hang from the ceiling—nobody wants to trip while handling the precious fossils!

When your parents were your age, people thought of dinosaurs as slow, dumb, and cold-blooded. Thanks to new fossil finds, new technologies, and new ways of studying prehistoric life, many ideas about dinosaurs have changed dramatically.

Scientists use trackways, comparisons to living animals, and computer models to learn about

Multi-million-year-old wood retrieved from Alberta's oil sands is so well preserved you can carve it. As Darren Tanke puts it, "If you can have pickled wood, you can potentially have pickled dinosaurs, and that would be the most amazing dinosaur find ever!"

dinosaurs as living animals. Investigations in dinosaur intelligence use a special x-ray—a computer tomography or CT scan—that lets scientists look inside dinosaur skulls. Powerful microscopes reveal tiny canals in fossilized bone where blood once flowed, canals that suggest that some dinosaurs grew as quickly as warm-blooded animals do today.

Studies of old dinosaur injuries might help resolve the debate about whether dinosaurs were warm-blooded (endothermic) or cold-blooded (ectothermic). If you sprain your ankle, the injured area gets warmer. This is only true for animals who are endothermic and can produce a fever. Using isotopic studies, researchers look for evidence of temperature rise at the wound sites of dinosaurs—a strong clue that dinosaurs were endotherms too!

GETTING TO THE HEART OF THE MATTER

Finding a dinosaur bone is always exciting. But imagine the thrill of discovering the world's first dinosaur heart! Using medical technology, scientists determined that the grapefruit-sized, reddish-brown clump of rock found in the chest cavity (see picture below) of a plant-eating dinosaur named *Thescelosaurus neglectus* was a 66-million-year-old dinosaur heart.

The research team used a computer tomography (CT) scanner to investigate the organ. CT scans use x-rays and computer software to visually "peel away" layers of tissue or, in this case, layers of dirt and fossilized bone. The computer-enhanced images suggest that the dinosaur, nicknamed Willo, has a four-chambered, double-pump heart that is more like yours than that of a lizard. Dr. Dale Russell, the Canadian palaeontologist who coordinated the study, says that Willo's heart provides an important piece of evidence that some dinosaurs were probably warm-blooded and as active as the birds and mammals we know today. You can see Willo's amazing heart at the North Carolina Museum of Natural Sciences in Raleigh.

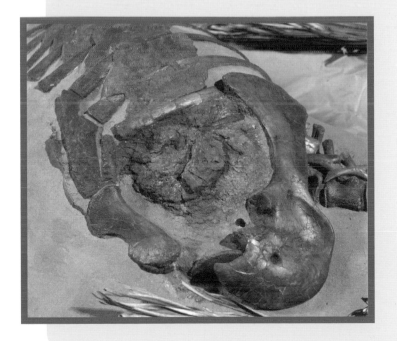

Tools of the Trade

What kinds of tools do you need to collect a dinosaur? Here are some of the tools palaeontologists and technicians take with them when they go into the field to excavate. Of course, like any travellers, they must be careful to pack only what they can successfully transport to the site. If they are working in another country, they may ship tools ahead of the trip, or depend on buying them when they arrive.

Jackhammer

1 The first challenge is to remove enough of the surrounding rock to see most of the specimen. This may be possible using shovels, pickaxes, or small pneumatic chisels. If there is a lot of ground cover and rock to get through, jackhammers and even bulldozers may be brought in to help.

Burlap for Jacket

3 Once the blocks are formed, it's time to start jacketing the top and sides of the fossils, to strengthen and protect them. First the fossil is lined with layers of moistened toilet paper. Then burlap strips dipped in plaster cover the bone. Now comes the tricky step of trenching underneath the bone until it is loose enough to roll over and wrap the other side, so the jacket covers the entire fossil.

Glue

2 The bones will usually be found cracked or broken. Various types of glue are used to penetrate cracks and seal the bones to prevent further damage. Next, trenches are dug to begin to outline the block of rock that will eventually be removed. The number and size of the blocks depends on the size of the specimens, and whether they will be carried out by people, trucks, or even helicopters.

Camera

4 During an excavation, careful records of the exact size, location, and orientation of each fossil and block is taken. Each is given its own field number. A quarry map is drawn to show the position of each fossil, and the entire site is photographed in detail. This information is vitally important to the researchers and technicians who will assemble and study the specimen back in the lab.

Dino Fact

Other tools used in the field include brushes of different sizes, a magnifying glass, and tiny chisels to help scientists reveal intricate parts of a fossil.

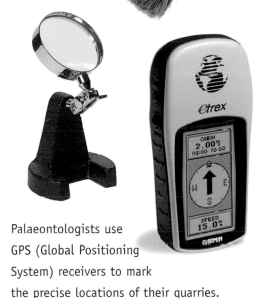

Palaeontologists use GPS (Global Positioning System) receivers to mark the precise locations of their quarries.

Meanwhile, Back in the Lab...

Fossil preparators use drills, chisels, hammers, and scrapers to remove fossils from the blocks of rock. Removing harder rocks is very time-consuming and expensive. The recent preparation of a *Chasmosaurus* skull (described on page 53) cost more than $3000 in carbide chisel points!

For smaller fossils contained in limestone, fossil preparators put down the tools and bring on the acid. Limestone (calcium carbonate) dissolves in acetic acid (vinegar). Fossil preparators immerse the limestone-covered fossils in an acetic acid bath—and then they wait. Eventually the rock will dissolve, leaving perfectly clean fossils. The next task is often to sort the hundreds, or even thousands, of small fossils released from the limestone back into a perfect 3-D puzzle.

Researcher Profile: Darren Tanke

When dinosaur technician Darren Tanke was a boy, he was crazy for dinosaurs. In fact, his earliest memories are of collecting rocks in the back alley behind his home in Calgary, Alberta. However, no one he knew thought that studying dinosaurs was a good career choice and he felt quite discouraged. Luckily, in his last year of high school, Darren was able to do a special study project on Alberta dinosaurs. Each week, he wrote a report on a different dinosaur species, and when he was finished, he had a 600-page book! He mailed it off to Philip Currie at the Royal Tyrrell Museum of Palaeontology, who was so impressed with the work, he invited Darren to join them as a volunteer. The very first afternoon Darren joined the team on a dig, he was able to identify rare skull fragments from a *Troodon* that he had researched for his report! Soon after, Philip offered him a seasonal job and Darren was on his way to a professional career as a technician at the Royal Tyrrell Museum.

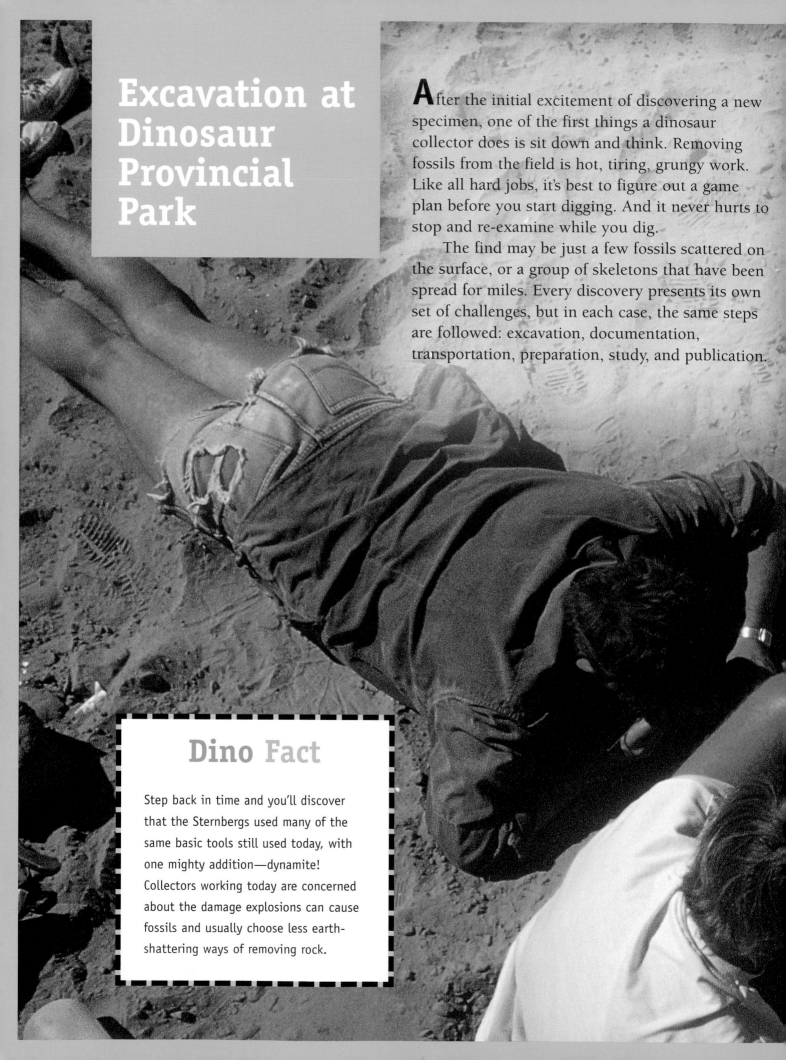

Excavation at Dinosaur Provincial Park

After the initial excitement of discovering a new specimen, one of the first things a dinosaur collector does is sit down and think. Removing fossils from the field is hot, tiring, grungy work. Like all hard jobs, it's best to figure out a game plan before you start digging. And it never hurts to stop and re-examine while you dig.

The find may be just a few fossils scattered on the surface, or a group of skeletons that have been spread for miles. Every discovery presents its own set of challenges, but in each case, the same steps are followed: excavation, documentation, transportation, preparation, study, and publication.

Dino Fact

Step back in time and you'll discover that the Sternbergs used many of the same basic tools still used today, with one mighty addition—dynamite! Collectors working today are concerned about the damage explosions can cause fossils and usually choose less earth-shattering ways of removing rock.

UNEARTHING THE PAST

This impressive image of a *Gorgosaurus* started with an excavation like the one shown here. From bones in rock, it takes a lot of work and study to put together an image of a dinosaur so realistic you can almost hear it roar.

DINOSAURS FROM COAST TO

If you were asked to choose a dinosaur mascot for your favourite Canadian sports team, you might be tempted to choose a hadrosaur (duckbill dinosaur). After all, in Canada scientists find more fossils from this group of dinosaurs than from any other. Horned dinosaurs, such as *Centrosaurus* or *Triceratops* would also make an excellent choice. There is no doubt that these large herbivorous, or plant-eating, dinosaurs were common residents of what is now Canada.

You wouldn't be wrong, however, if you took your cue from the Toronto Raptors, and selected a fierce carnivorous (meat-eating) dinosaur. There is plenty of fossil evidence to support the idea that giant tyrannosaurs thrived in Canada, and that smaller (human-sized) meat-eating dinosaurs, the theropods, were also present.

Just because a dinosaur was found in Canada, that doesn't mean it lived everywhere in the country. Just like animals today, different kinds of dinosaurs thrived in different habitats. Figuring out where dinosaurs once lived is especially difficult because many environments were not good for fossilization. Dinosaurs that lived in these places might never have been preserved. Even if they were preserved, the rock in which they were buried might be covered by cities or forests, or carved away by glaciers.

In the following pages, you'll meet some of the carnivorous and herbivorous dinosaurs that lived in Canada. You'll also get an "insider's peek" at the creative ways Canadian palaeontologists and their colleagues discover what dinosaurs were like when they were living, breathing animals.

COAST TO COAST

TYRANNOSAURS
Leader of the Pack

▲
When you were born, less than a dozen partial *Tyrannosaurus rex* skeletons had ever been found. Today, almost twice as many exist for study. Each new discovery is changing the way palaeontologists view the dinosaur that thrives in so many people's imaginations.

Tyrannosaurus *rex* is the world's most popular dinosaur. It's not surprising—even among animals alive today, the big carnivores, or meat-eaters, have the ability to thrill and fascinate us.

Just how social were tyrannosaurids? Evidence of pack behaviour of this group of dinosaurs is growing. A *T. rex* quarry in the United States contained four adults; a *Gigantosaurus* bone bed in Patagonia had half a dozen animals in it.

When the Alberta bone bed where Barnum Brown discovered nine *Albertosaurus* in 1910 was re-opened in 1998, the discovery of four more *Albertosaurus* increased the size of the pack to thirteen individuals. And the more Philip Currie (see Profile on page 39) and his team digs, the more they find! The *Albertosaurus* bone bed contains adults and juveniles, and the remains of a duckbill *Hypacrosaurus*.

Was it a pack of *Albertosaurus*? Tim Tokaryk (see Profile on page 43) suggests that *T. rex* may have lived a mostly solitary life, much like present-day hunters like tigers, whereas *Albertosaurus* may have lived in prides or packs like lions.

It is hard to imagine a force great enough to kill fourteen *Albertosaurus* at the same time, but scientists get clues from the environment. The fossilized wood around the bones may tell the story of a major flood that sent both dinosaurs and trees tumbling to their deaths. The survival of delicate bones provides further evidence that the dinosaurs were not killed by predators. Maybe the *Albertosaurus* were chasing the *Hypacrosaurus* when the flood occurred, or the *Hypacrosaurus* was crossing the river when the waters rose. The excavation is still underway, and with each new bone comes more information.

DINO PROFILE

Albertosaurus

- Age: Late Cretaceous, about 72 mya
- Location in Canada: Alberta
- Size: 9 m (29 ft) long
- Likely diet: Hadrosaurs (duckbill dinosaurs)
- Special discovery: The "pack" of 13 *Albertosaurus* that Philip Currie and his team are currently studying was first discovered by Barnum Brown in 1910. It was Alberta's first big dinosaur dig.
- Current debate: Were *Albertosaurus* packs led by a dominant female, as elephant herds are today?
  It's difficult to determine a fossil skeleton's gender, but some scientists believe that female *Albertosaurus* had one less tail vertebra than the male, presumably to make birthing easier. The "missing vertebra" skeletons are bigger, leading to the idea that packs of *Albertosaurus* were led by bigger, female dinosaurs.

▲

Not all dinosaur excavations go as planned. When a helicopter tried to lift the sacrum (the heaviest part of the backbone) of the *Hypacrosaurus* from the *Albertosaurus* bone bed, the weight proved to be too great. The plaster-jacketed bone started to swing, threatening to crash the helicopter, and the pilot had no choice but to cut it loose. Smashed to smithereens!

Tyrannosaurs
Cheeky Behaviour

▲
Late Cretaceous, about 67 million years ago in what is now eastern Wyoming. Here a *Tyrannosaurus rex* brings down an *Edmontosaurus*. Tooth marks in the broken and later healed tailbones of an adult *Edmontosaurus* prove that the duckbill dinosaurs sometimes survived predatory *T. rex* attacks.

Chomp! What's big enough to bite the head of a huge, meat-eating dinosaur? Another huge meat-eating dinosaur! Nearly half of the skulls from tyrannosaurid dinosaurs in Alberta, such as *Albertosaurus*, *Gorgosaurus*, and *Tyrannosaurus*, show evidence of healing bites on their faces.

Why were tyrannosaurids biting each other's faces? Philip Currie and Darren Tanke (see Profile on page 31) looked at fossilized skulls and the behaviour of living

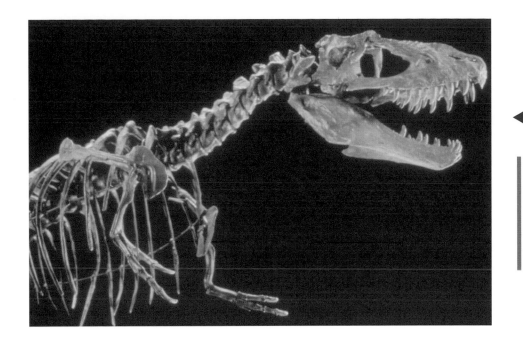

Who would win if *Tyrannosaurus rex* and *Albertosaurus* got into a head-biting duel? Nobody, because the duel could never happen. *T. rex* lived millions of years after *Albertosaurus* (like this skeleton at the Royal Tyrrell Museum) became extinct.

animals to help them solve this riddle. They knew that some large predators, such as tigers, roar and bite when defending their territories. Could tyrannosaurid dinosaurs be defending territories? Or did the bite marks result from courtship and mating injuries? Male sea otters, for instance, often bite and bloody the noses of females when they are breeding.

Many of the bites were severe, ruling out the idea that tyrannosaurids were play-biting like young puppies. Instead, Philip and Darren suspect that the bites were some sort of aggressive social interaction, with the animals facing off and gnawing each other. Some of the bites were so fierce, one

tyrannosaur sports a souvenir tooth from another embedded in its jaw.

Tyrannosaurids appear to have fought throughout their lives, as younger individuals have more face-biting injuries than adults. Perhaps these smaller individuals were more likely to have been attacked by others their age, as well as by larger adults.

Researcher Profile: Philip Currie

When he was six years old, Philip Currie found a plastic dinosaur in a box of cereal. His parents had to buy a lot of cereal so he could collect the whole set! In grade five, he found a book in his classroom called *All About Dinosaurs*, and read what it was like to be a dinosaur hunter. He decided then and there to become a palaeontologist. Today, he is a professor at the University of Alberta, and is recognized around the world as a leading palaeontologist.

TYRANNOSAURS
The Big Bad

▲

Bite-force studies confirm that tyrannosaurs had incredible jaw strength— each *T. rex* tooth could exert a crushing force equal to the weight of a pickup truck.

How did a *T. rex* eat? Scar marks on tyrannosaur skulls illustrate the tremendous size of the neck muscles needed to get its enormous teeth in and out of prey. Just imagine the horrific sight of a feeding tyrannosaur—long, sharp teeth, and mouth running red with bloodstained saliva! Tyrannosaurs may have delivered a bone-deep bite and then waited for their prey to bleed to death.

The serrated teeth served a grisly purpose. The teeth of Indonesia's komodo dragons (the world's largest living lizards) are remarkably similar in structure to those of tyrannosaurs. Each time a komodo dragon chomps down and releases, meat clings to the serrations on its teeth. As the meat rots, bacteria grow, creating a poisonous bite.

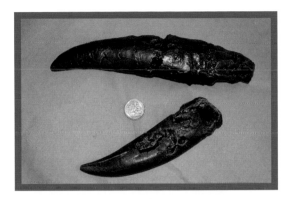

▲

The fearsome teeth of *T. rex* might look like steak knives, but recent research suggests that they might have functioned less as knives than like pegs, gripping the food as the tyrannosaur pulled it to pieces.

DINO PROFILE

Tyrannosaurus rex

- Age: 65 mya
- Location in Canada: Alberta, Saskatchewan
- Size: 12.2 m (40 ft) long.
- Likely diet: *Triceratops* (horned) and *Edmontosaurus* (duckbill) dinosaurs
- Special discovery: "Scotty," discovered in Eastend, Saskatchewan, in 1991, is only the second *T. rex* found in Canada.
- Current debate: Was *T. rex* a predator or a scavenger?
  Gnawed bones and shed tooth crowns among *Edmontosaurus* that died in natural disasters show that *T. rex* was an effective scavenger, and it's likely that it could attack live prey too.

TRACE EVIDENCE

Fossilized dinosaur "poop," or coprolites, are rare treasures that reveal a lot about what dinosaurs ate. In 1997, Karen Chin was able to prove that a 6.8 kg (15 lb) fossil found near the skeleton of Scotty, the Saskatchewan *T. rex* (see page 42), was indeed the first confirmed *T. rex* coprolite. It was chock-full of pulverized bone, which turned out to be from a young herbivorous dinosaur, most likely a *Triceratops* or *Edmontosaurus*.

WANT TO RACE?

How fast could a huge tyrannosaur move? Eric Snively, a palaeontologist at the University of Calgary, believes tyrannosaurs were great sprinters. He used CT scans (special x-rays) and 3-D computer enhancement to study the structure of *Albertosaurus* feet and concluded that the faster the dinosaur ran, the more the foot ligaments would tighten. The tighter foot ligaments meant that a running tyrannosaur was likely quite agile. Giant "drumstick" muscles (extending from the crest at the knee) and large hips suggest that tyrannosaurs had fast acceleration, perhaps reaching speeds close to 50 km (31 miles) per hour.

Finding Scotty in Saskatchewan

▲

**Unearthing the big bad!
Technicians are dwarfed by a
Tyrannosaurus rex skeleton as
they slowly remove the
overlying rock from it.**

Tim Tokaryk is a palaeontologist and bookstore
owner in Eastend, Saskatchewan. He sees
palaeontologists as "historians of the past" and is
curious about the people who picked up, pondered,
pocketed, and transported fossils years before he was
born.

People from other parts of Canada working for
the boundary commission and, later, the Geological
Survey of Canada were responsible for much of
Saskatchewan's early fossil exploration. Harold S.
"Corky" Jones, a cowpoke from a ranch near Eastend,
became Saskatchewan's first resident palaeontologist.
Corky had a passion for not only finding fossils, but
also for discovering their significance. He set up a

small museum in the early 1900s that exists to this day.

Like Corky, Tim Tokaryk knows the excitement of discovery—the thrilling discovery of the first *Tyrannosaurus rex* skeleton in Saskatchewan! His team spotted "Scotty" the *T. rex* in 1991 while on a prospecting trip for the Royal Saskatchewan Museum. Tim returned to the site and began excavation in 1994, when the discovery of a tooth within a socket and other fossil remains suggested that the rest of the skeleton was likely to be found nearby.

Finding the skeleton was lucky; removing it from the ground has been pure hard work. Unlike Sue, the world's best *T. rex* specimen (discovered in South Dakota in 1990), Scotty looked, according to Tim, like a "regurgitated omelette." The carcass had washed downstream after the dinosaur died and, as it started to rot, trees and leaves were trapped against its bones. The bones themselves were flipped and scattered by the current. As a result, none of the fossil bones are joined together and many of them are stacked on top of one another.

▲

Sometimes the job of removing the skeleton is tough, as the fossil bones can be virtually cemented into the stone where they were found. In some cases, the only way to tell where the rock ends and the fossil begins is under a microscope back at the lab. You can watch how difficult it is to prepare Scotty's skeleton at the T. rex Discovery Centre. Two-thirds of the entire skeleton has been recovered, and more is still to come.

Researcher Profile: Tim Tokaryk

Tim Tokaryk learned the importance of volunteering from his grandmother. As a young museum volunteer, he remembers sneaking out of math class to spend afternoons at the museum. Unfortunately for Tim, his math teacher's wife worked at the museum and quickly alerted her husband! Today Tim is supervisor of the Royal Saskatchewan Museum Fossil Research Station at the T. rex Discovery Centre in Eastend, Saskatchewan.

THEROPODS
The Canada–China Connection

Dino Fact

Spend a day at the beach and you'll find sand sticking to every part of your body—sand in your ears, sand in your eyelashes, even sand in your belly button! Sand traces every fold and crevice of your body. Millions of years ago, the semi-arid environment of Mongolia was ideal for sandstorms. Suffocated and then buried by swirling sand, many dinosaurs have been preserved in exquisite detail.

▲

One of Mongolia's most fascinating fossil discoveries is of a *Velociraptor* locked in combat with a *Protoceratops*. Both creatures probably died instantly in a sandstorm.

Canada is a great place to find big meat-eaters like *Gorgosaurus* and *Tyrannosaurus rex*. But it isn't a very good place to find the smaller carnivores, theropods. Many species are known only from a single skull and a couple of toe bones. Perhaps these "snack sized" dinosaurs were hunted and eaten. Or maybe their light skeletons were broken apart and washed away by the big rivers that helped bury and fossilize their larger cousins. In either case, Philip Currie (see Profile on page 39) has discovered that a good way to understand the lives of Canada's small meat-eaters is to study their closest relatives in places where they are better preserved—China and the Gobi Desert of Mongolia!

Philip Currie believes strongly in the value of palaeontologists from different countries working together to understand the prehistoric world. In 1984, he co-led The Canada–China Dinosaur Project, the largest dinosaur hunt in history. Teams of Canadian and Chinese scientists searched for dinosaur skeletons, eggs, fossils, and tracks in both countries for five summers. Driven by the desire to trace the relationships between various groups of dinosaurs in Asia and North America, their findings have changed the way we look at dinosaurs. Together, they discovered eleven new species of dinosaurs and countless other spectacular finds.

Velociraptor, the now-famous dinosaur from central Asia, was almost identical to a small theropod from North America named *Ornitholestes* (see below). By studying the well-preserved fossil remains of *Velociraptor* and other Central Asian theropods, Philip Currie and his colleagues from North America and China are piecing together the lives of Canada's small predatory dinosaurs.

▼

DINO PROFILE

Velociraptor

- Age: 67 mya
- Location: central Asia
- Size: 3 m (6 ft) long
- Likely diet: meat (probably hunted in packs for other dinosaurs)
- Special discovery: Thanks to the movie *Jurassic Park*, this little theropod is a world-famous dinosaur. *Velociraptor* (whose name means "swift robber") was actually smaller than shown in the film, and it had a longer, thinner snout. An effective killing machine—light and fast—it had on each inside toe a banana-sized hooked claw that could snap down, slicing deeply into its victims.
- Current debate: Did *Velociraptor* have feathers?
  Velociraptor is a dromaeosaurid dinosaur. The recent discovery of feathers on another dromaeosaurid named *Sinornithosaurus* has led some scientists to argue that many, if not most, of the meat eating dinosaurs were feathered.

◀

On a visit to the Gobi Desert of Mongolia, palaeontologists set up camp, complete with the flags of China and Canada.

THEROPODS
Dream of Feathers

▲

Sinosauropteryx prima translates as "first Chinese dragon feather." The fossilized skeleton shows the long tail and flexibility that would have made it a fast hunter.

Imagine finally seeing something you had long hoped for but never thought possible. Philip Currie did just that in 1996, when he laid eyes on a small theropod dinosaur at the National Geological Museum of China. What was so unforgettable about it was what surrounded the body—feathers!

The idea that birds descended from dinosaurs was first put forward by Thomas Huxley in the 1860s when he compared *Megalosaurus* (a giant theropod dinosaur) with an ostrich, listing 35 features that the two groups shared. The idea remained unpopular for the next hundred years until John Ostrom, a palaeontologist at Yale University, began building a bone-by-bone case for the link between *Archaeopteryx* (the earliest known bird) and theropod dinosaurs.

Feathers are extremely fragile and usually disappear without leaving any fossilized trace. So John Ostrom never expected to see direct proof of his theory. When he first saw photographs of the feathered dinosaur, he was flabbergasted: "I was really in a state of shock. I did not think my legs would hold me up."

A Flurry of Feathered Dinosaurs

The first feathered dinosaur, *Sinosauropteryx prima* ("first Chinese dragon feather"), was discovered in 1996 in the Liaoning fossil beds of Northeast China. Since that first exciting day in 1996, five species of "feathered" dinosaurs have been discovered in Liaoning province. Philip Currie believes many more will be described in the years ahead.

The five species are all theropods, or meat-eating dinosaurs, but they represent five different family histories that are as different from one another as cats, dogs, bears, and weasels are today. The fact that dinosaurs from such different stocks all had feathers suggests that many meat-eating dinosaurs were probably feathered.

Horns, Frills, Spikes... and Feathers!

Dinosaurs were highly visual animals that evolved a fantastic array of crests, frills, and horns to attract mates, warn potential rivals, and communicate a dinosaur's position within its social group. Once dinosaurs had acquired feathers for insulation, what could be more natural than to adapt them into display structures? Feathers may also have played an important role in dinosaur parenting. Specimens of *Oviraptor* (a small theropod dinosaur) have been found on nests of eggs, and their positions suggest that long feathers on the backs of their arms might have helped the dinosaurs protect and warm the eggs.

Most scientists agree that the blue jay–sized *Archaeopteryx* (the earliest known bird), which lived 150 million years ago, is the dividing line between dinosaurs and birds.

THEROPODS
Birds of a Feather

▲

Palaeontologists were cutting a large block of sandstone out of the valley floor when their jackhammer penetrated the shoulder-bone of a dinosaur fossil. This excavation site is where they found the *Ornithomimus* skeleton.

It looks like a small stain on a rock, but to palaeontologists it's a significant discovery—the first beak from a carnivorous dinosaur! Discovered in 1996 in the Devil's Coulee, in the Red Deer River badlands of Alberta, this rare fossil was unearthed just as the debate about the relationship between dinosaurs and birds was really heating up.

When Dennis Braman (see Profile on page 13) and Kevin Aulenback (a technician) unexpectedly found a dinosaur fossil, they immediately called Philip Currie (see Profile on page 39). It was the first complete skeleton of a small, ostrich-like ornithomimid dinosaur to turn up in Canada in more than 60 years.

Given the excellent preservation of the skeleton, Philip and his colleagues dared to hope that the skull might turn out to be complete. Dinosaur skulls, even those from large, heavy dinosaurs, are frequently carried off by predators or crushed flat during the process of fossilization. The chance of such a delicate, lightweight skull surviving intact are even more remote. In this case, the entire skull was present. It was as thin as a dime in places, yet it had survived 75 million years.

In the rare cases where an ornithomimid skull has been unearthed, it has always been lacking the beak. Beaks are composed of keratin, the same material found in bird feathers and your fingernails. The keratinous stain in the sandstone along the edges of the dinosaur's lower and upper jaws proves that a beak was once present.

Using a CT scan (special x-ray) at Calgary's Foothills Hospital, palaeontologists made a 3-D computerized image of the skull, inside and out—a skull that looks just like a bird's!

DINO PROFILE

Dromaeosaurus

- Age: 76–74 mya
- Location in Canada: Alberta
- Size: large-dog sized, with short arms and a very long tail
- Likely diet: meat
- Special discovery: The first fossils of *Dromaeosaurus* were discovered by Barnum Brown on the banks of the Red Deer River, in Alberta, in 1914.
- Current debate: Did *Dromaeosaurus* hunt in packs?
  Several isolated finds indicate the presence of *Dromaeosaurus* teeth among the bones of much larger dinosaurs. Packs of dromaeosaurs might have attacked larger animals, or the teeth could have simply washed into the fossil sites of the bigger beasts.

▲ Try this to get a close look at what a theropod dinosaur skeleton (like this dromaeosaur) looked like. Next time you have a turkey dinner, save the skeleton. Boil it down in a pot, scrape off the leftover meat, and you've got the makings of a 3-D dinosaur jigsaw puzzle.

▲ By the time duckbill and horned dinosaurs were roaming Alberta, the types of birds you'd discover would look fairly familiar. Ancient relatives of shorebirds, seabirds, and others familiar to us today were all around millions of years before the last dinosaurs disappeared. Birds like this Hesperornis ("western bird") from the Late Cretaceous (80–65 million years ago) were very loon-like, but with one big difference—they had teeth!

The Collections Area of the CMN

It's all in the numbers. 1929, 1924, 1915…can you spot the dates on the jacketed bones in this picture? Many of these plaster jackets contain dinosaurs collected by the Sternbergs and others during the Great Canadian Dinosaur Rush. But this is not a historic photo. It was taken in the Collections Area of the Canadian Museum of Nature in 2003! Preparing dinosaur skeletons for study or display is so expensive and time-consuming, the shelves of many major museums are piled high with decades-old plaster jackets still waiting to be opened.

The "section" and "box" numbers on the jackets provide valuable information about where the fossils they contain were found. Collections managers keep careful records of each of these numbers, and of the field notes that might have been written when the fossils were found. Scientists working at different institutions all over the world use these records to search for a particular specimen, just as you can search a library catalogue to find a particular book. Like a grabbag of wrapped presents, jackets may hold delightful surprises. That's just what happened when a team of Canadian Museum of Nature scientists opened a 1958 jacket—and discovered a brand new dinosaur! Turn the page and read all about it.

CERATOPSIANS
A New Horned Dinosaur

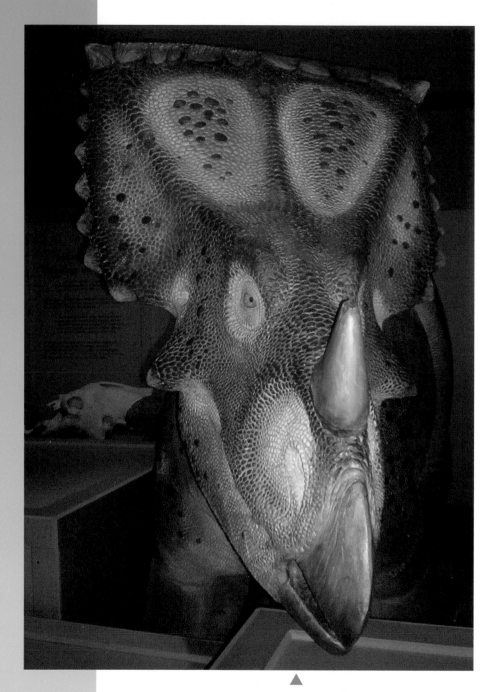

The newly discovered *Chasmosaurus irvinensis* skeleton is now the "holotype," which means it is the first specimen of that species to be scientifically described. The skeleton becomes the most important reference for palaeontologists who study these dinosaurs. The Canadian Museum of Nature possesses holotypes for two of the three other known chasmosaurs, and its collection of horned dinosaurs is one of the best in the world.

You don't have to travel to the badlands to make important dinosaur discoveries. Dr. Robert Holmes and a team of scientists recently discovered a brand new species of dinosaur in the piles of jacketed bones in the Canadian Museum of Nature's collections area.

It can take one person as long as you have been alive to prepare a single dinosaur skeleton. So the collections areas of many museums are filled with specimens just waiting to be prepared.

The new species of dinosaur that Robert "discovered" was originally collected in 1958 by Dr. Wann Langston, a palaeontologist formerly with the Canadian Museum of Nature. According to Wann's original field notes, the plaster jacket contained a fairly complete skeleton of a horned dinosaur named *Chasmosaurus belli*. The jacketed bones remained unopened for more than thirty years.

Around the time you were born, there was a big debate about the position of the limbs of horned dinosaurs. The rear limbs were upright like those of an elephant or a cow; however, the front limbs seemed to point out to the side like those of a turtle. Many scientists thought this posture didn't seem right. Wann Langston remembered that the specimen of *Chasmosaurus belli* he had collected in 1958 had died sort of standing up, and he suggested it might provide some clues.

When the museum preparators began cutting off the plaster jacket, they realized they had it upside down and were opening the skull side first. And—surprise!—they found something new.

The scientists noticed that the skull was different from those of the three other known chasmosaur species. The team set to work carefully reconstructing and measuring all aspects of the skull. The dimensions and details were then compared with other known ceratopsian dinosaurs. The results were conclusive—a brand new dinosaur, *Chasmosaurus irvinensis*, was named.

A TRULY CANADIAN NAME

The name *Chasmosaurus irvinensis* was an obvious choice, according to Kieran Shepherd, the Canadian Museum of Nature's Chief Collections Manager for Earth Sciences. This dinosaur was discovered in Canada, worked on by a Canadian-based research team, and details were published in a Canadian journal. The name recognizes the local community of Irvine, Alberta, where the dinosaur was found.

▲

Compared with the other known chasmosaur species (see above), the skull of *Chasmosaurus irvinensis* (at left) has a squarer frill with bony bits at the top, and the holes or "chasms" are smaller.

|53|

CERATOPSIANS
Spikes and Frills

▲

Although *Triceratops* are famous the world over, the fossil record is comprised almost entirely of skulls and isolated skeletal bones. In fact, the mounted skeletons of *Triceratops* you see on display in museums (like this one at the Tyrrell) are made from the bones of at least two, and often more, individuals.

If you watch old dinosaur movies, you're sure to see a *Triceratops* fighting off a tyrannosaur with its long, pointy nose horn. Today, palaeontologists think the wonderful array of horns and frills found on ceratopsians or horned dinosaurs were used for much more than simple defence.

Take a look at ants, chameleons, deer, sheep, or cattle, and you'll notice that lots of living animals have horns, antlers, or other similar structures. In each case, the primary function of these structures is to help the animal attract and compete for mates. Scott Sampson, a Canadian-born palaeontologist now working at the Utah Museum of Natural History, looks to living animals as well as the fossil record to argue that ceratopsian frills and horns served the same purpose.

It's easy to recognize the dominant ram in a herd of mountain sheep by his impressive, curved horns. Like young mountain sheep, young ceratopsians did not have fully developed horns and frills until they reached adult size. The size and shape of horns and frills likely provided information about the age and status of individual dinosaurs to other members of the group.

Scott believes that horned dinosaurs were social animals that lived, at least part of the year, in organized groups. Those with smaller horns, like *Chasmosaurus*, were probably more sociable, relying on large herds to deal with predators. *Triceratops*, on the other hand, had enormous horns, and the fossil evidence suggests these dinosaurs were more solitary

DO WE REALLY KNOW *TRICERATOPS*?

Palaeontologists are currently preparing a fairly rare skeleton—a *Triceratops*! The specimen is nicknamed Kelsey, after the granddaughter of the couple who discovered the skull on their ranch near Newcastle, Wyoming, in 1998. Kelsey is one of the most complete *Triceratops* skeletons to be collected to date. Its spectacularly well-preserved skull measures 2 m (6.5 ft) long!

DINO **P**ROFILE

Triceratops

- Age: 65 mya
- Location in Canada: Alberta, Saskatchewan
- Size: 9 m (30 ft) long
- Likely diet: plants
- Special discovery: *Triceratops* may have been among the last dinosaurs on Earth. *Triceratops* fossils are found at the boundary that marks the end of the Cretaceous period.
- Current debate: Did *Triceratops* sprawl or run with legs straight beneath their bodies? There are so few complete *Triceratops* to study, scientists look to other ceratopsians, such as *Chasmosaurus*, to help them answer this question.

▲

Some adult *Styracosaurus* frills had longer spikes than others. Were the "big spiked" individuals males? Some palaeontologists think so but, so far, no one knows for sure.

CERATOPSIANS
Living Together and Dying Together

▲

Pointing out a *Centrosaurus* vertebra (backbone) among the thousands of bones found in Dinosaur Provincial Park. The bone bed spans an area the size of a football field, and in some places there are 60 bones in a space no bigger than a sidewalk square.

DINO PROFILE

Centrosaurus

- Age: 76–74 mya
- Location in Canada: Alberta
- Size: 6 m (20 ft) long
- Likely diet: plants
- Special discovery: Several mass death sites, containing large numbers of *Centrosaurus*, have been found in various parts of southern Alberta.
- Current debate: How quickly would a baby *Centrosaurus*, small enough to fit in a grapefruit-sized egg, grow into an adult the length of a bus?
  No one knows for sure, though investigations of juvenile-through-adult bones from another horned dinosaur, *Psittacosaurus*, indicate that they reached adult size in eight or nine years.

Palaeontologists often feel lucky when they find a single dinosaur bone. Imagine the excitement of finding a bone bed where hundreds, if not thousands, of dinosaurs died at the same time. That's what Philip Currie (see Profile on page 39) and his team experienced in the late 1970s, when they discovered a mass concentration of *Centrosaurus* (a horned dinosaur) bones in Dinosaur Provincial Park.

The fact that so many *Centrosaurus* died together at the same time gives scientists a rare chance to study dinosaur social life. By comparing the same bones, such as the right femur (upper leg bone) from many individuals, it appears that the group was made up of different-sized and, therefore, different-aged *Centrosaurus*. Some of the smallest bones are so tiny, it's impossible for Michael Ryan to determine whether the individuals had hatched or were still in their eggs. In addition to these very young animals, there are bones from older, mature animals.

Did *Centrosaurus* live in herds all year round? Or did they gather during a season that sometimes coincided with killer storms? And why haven't hadrosaur (duckbill) bone beds been found in the same environment? (Hadrosaurs are believed to have grouped together, and made up 50 percent of the total dinosaur population of that environment.) The fun thing about palaeontology, according to Michael, is that there's always more questions like these to answer.

SOME DEATHS ARE STRANGER THAN FICTION

Darren Tanke (see Profile on page 31) has an unusual collection. He collects true accounts of mass animal deaths, to help him better interpret bone beds and other instances where many dinosaurs died together. Darren's collection includes tales of schools of fish beaching themselves while chasing prey; of 50 caribou hit by lightning; and of cloud-icing events that caused ducks and geese to literally rain from the sky. But more ordinary events can also cause high mortality. A wildebeest can drown or be trampled when water dropping from the backs of the other wildebeest crossing a river ahead of it make the riverbank too slippery to climb.

Researcher Profile: Michael Ryan

Michael Ryan can't remember a time when he did not want to study dinosaurs. In grade five he surprised his parents by turning their basement into a dinosaur museum, using his collection of plastic dinosaur models, fossils, and hand-made dioramas and posters. Michael grew up in Ottawa, home of the Canadian Museum of Nature, and he spent many weekends sketching the skeletons. This eventually led to him receiving degrees in biology and education, and working for the Royal Tyrrell Museum of Palaeontology. Michael is now the Curator and Head of Vertebrate Paleontology at the Cleveland Museum of Natural History.

Alberta's Famous Centrosaurus Beds

Dozens of *Centrosaurus* bone beds found within a small area are suggesting to palaeontologists that these horned dinosaurs spent some quality time together.

Since the 1970s, more than two dozen *Centrosaurus* bone beds have been discovered across southern Alberta. The fact that bones from one type of dinosaur appear within the same 20-metre (65-foot) thick rock layer is strong evidence that *Centrosaurus* came together in very large numbers and that something caused them to undergo a mass death.

Michael Ryan (see Profile on page 57) believes that whatever caused the mass death was big. Other bone beds containing other dinosaurs—duckbills, ankylosaurs, ornithomimids, theropods—have also been discovered from the same time.

Working closely with David Eberth, a sedimentologist/palaeoecologist (scientist who studies the formation and ecology of ancient environments), Michael concludes that the mass killer may have been a giant wave called a tsunami. Every 200 years or so, enormous storms might have come in and completely devastated the plains; drowning everything that lived there.

Michael's theory has replaced Philip Currie's initial thoughts that the dinosaurs drowned while trying to cross a river in flood. Tens of thousands of caribou had died in just that way in northern Quebec the same year that Philip was first publishing scientific papers about the *Centrosaurus* bone bed.

Researcher Profile: Wendy Sloboda

TRACE EVIDENCE

In 1987, Wendy Sloboda, then a teenaged dinosaur enthusiast, found eggshells near the small town of Warner, Alberta. The Royal Tyrrell Museum of Palaeontology quickly sent out a crew. It wasn't long before Kevin Aulenback, a technician with the museum, uncovered not only an egg, but a dinosaur embryo (see photo below)! In the more than 20 years since the discovery of the *Centrosaurus* bone bed, Wendy's find is one of many large fossil concentrations. Thousands of bones from dinosaurs that had not yet hatched, as well as hundreds of eggs, have been recovered.

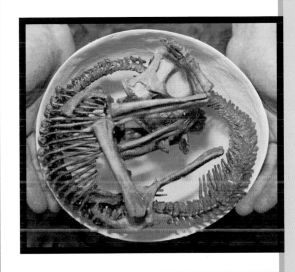

Wendy Sloboda was just a teenager when she found dinosaur eggshells in Alberta. She still isn't very tall, and her husband teases her that being "close to the ground" is why she's so good at finding fossils. The real secret, says Wendy, is knowing how to look. Wendy is a dinosaur technician and prospector who works with scientists in Alberta and all over the world.

SAUROPODS
Size Matters

As intimidating as their size may have been, these *Brachiosaurus* weren't vicious meat-eaters—they preferred to nibble the leaves that no other dinosaur could ever reach.

Although many types of dinosaurs were your height or smaller, there's something about the REALLY BIG ones that captures your heart and imagination. Sauropods were the largest animals ever to walk on Earth. With long necks that dwarfed those of modern-day giraffes, and legs bigger than any elephant's, these creatures are the ultimate example of what makes dinosaurs so captivating.

Sauropod discovery really took off in the 1970s when the size of finds went from giant to truly humongous. Discovered in 1972, the *Supersaurus* was the largest dinosaur ever, at 40 metres (130 feet) long. Eight years later, palaeontologists unearthed a tall *Ultrasaurus* that could crane its neck more than 9 metres (30 feet) above even *Supersaurus*! So what qualifies a dinosaur as the biggest ever? Here are the current record-holders:

• **Length**

About the time that you were born, a New Mexico team found a sauropod even bigger than *Supersaurus* or *Ultrasaurus*. Named *Seismosaurus* or "Quake Lizard," this enormous animal was as long as a passenger jet, with an estimated length of between 37 and 52 metres (120 and 170 feet).

• **Height**

The record for height currently sits with *Sauroposeiden*. This "Lizard Earthquake God" has the longest neck in the fossil record. Individual vertebrae (neck bones) are as tall as a typical eight-year-old child. If reconstructions prove accurate, it could top 18 metres (60 feet) in height.

• **Weight**

Argentinosaurus, discovered in 1993, could have balanced on a see-saw with a blue whale; leaving scientists to ponder why didn't this dinosaur collapse under its own weight?

STUDYING DINOSAUR GROWTH

Whether it's your toe bone or the toe bone of a *T. rex*, all bones grow and change. Histologists (scientists who study bone) examine thin slices of dinosaur bone under magnification, and have determined growth rates for a number of different dinosaurs. Many types of dinosaurs grew a lot like you—fast growth when you are young that slows and stops when you reach adulthood.

• *Maiasaura* may have grown as tall as a basketball hoop in its first year.

• The giant sauropod *Apatosaurus* may have grown from a 2-metre (6.5 ft) hatchling to a 30-metre (100-ft) adult the length of a public swimming pool in 10–16 years.

• Human-sized *Troodon* may have reached adult size in 3–5 years. That's a much faster growth rate than yours!

Researcher Profile: Hans-Dieter Sues

Hans grew up in Europe where large, untouched dinosaur sites were difficult to come by. His passion for looking for fossils along road cuts or behind McDonald's dumpsters has served him well. He has discovered a number of new species by looking in unusual places. He was Vice-President, Collections and Research at the Royal Ontario Museum, and is now Associate Director for Research and Collections, at the Smithsonian's National Museum of Natural History.

SAUROPODS
Solving Mysteries

Dino Fact

Many of the sauropod skeletons found just since you were born weigh five times what scientists thought the biggest sauropod was 30 or 40 years ago. Do bigger ones remain to be found? Perhaps you'll be the one to discover a dinosaur larger than anyone could imagine.

When the giant sauropod *Diplodocus carnegie* was unearthed in 1877, casts of its spectacular skeleton were shipped to museums around the world. Each enormous leg was positioned straight beneath the body, just like the limbs of a horse. But not everyone agreed on the leg placement. German palaeontologists argued that the legs should sprawl out to the sides— these heavyweight dinosaurs had to live in lakes where the water could support their tremendous weight. Who was right? The mystery was solved in the 1940s when scientists found an impressive dinosaur trackway in the western United States. The metre-long footprints could only have been made by a sauropod. The narrow space between the left and right prints confirmed that sauropods did indeed walk with their legs straight beneath their bodies. Furthermore, the placement of the tracks suggested that sauropods might actually have avoided water.

Dinosaur posture is an important clue to telling sauropods apart. The brachiosaurids (like *Brachiosaurus, Sauroposeidon,* and *Ultrasaurus*) held their heads high. It's easy to imagine them nibbling leaves from trees, just as giraffes do today. Other sauropods (like *Diplodocus*) held their necks almost parallel to the ground. Poke a long, slender stick into a bush or pond and you'll get a sense of how these sauropods might have used their long necks to reach foliage in forests too dense or wetlands too muddy for their bodies to enter.

Different types of sauropods held their necks in different postures. The *Diplodocus* (large dinosaur in picture to left) held its neck fairly parallel to the ground. After assembling the skeleton of a *Mamenchiasaurus* (above) found in China, Canadian scientists found that it also held its neck horizontal most of the time, not straight up as shown here.

DINO PROFILE

Sauroposeidon

- Age: 112–97 mya
- Location: Oklahoma, U.S.A.
- Size: 30.5 m (100 ft) long
- Likely diet: plants
- Special discovery: This dinosaur may have had the longest neck of any land animal. Each neck bone was about your height—about 120 centimetres (4 ft) long—and was so massive, they were first thought to be prehistoric trees! A CT-scan (special x-ray) of the fossils reveals that the massive bones were filled with tiny air cells that lightened the load the creature had to carry.
- Current debate: What was the largest animal ever to have lived on land? In 2001, a villager walking through a canyon in Argentina's southern Patagonia came upon the neck bones of what may be the biggest dinosaur yet. Scientists estimate the length of this giant at 48–50 m (157–167 ft)!

A BIG, BIG NEWSFLASH

Sauropods had never been found in Canada—at least before 2002. Thanks to his passion for looking for footprints, Richard McCrea (see Profile on page 68) has made a remarkable discovery—several footprints and a trackway of sauropod dinosaurs in British Columbia! More unique still, the footprints are accompanied by fossil bones. This is the first proof positive that the footsteps of giant sauropods once shook Canadian soil. Stay tuned for more details as the excavation of this remarkable site progresses.

Down-East Dinosaur Hunting

Dino Fact

About 200 million years ago, Earth's land masses were joined together into a super-continent called Pangaea. Prosauropod remains have been found on nearly every continent now, which suggests that prosauropod dinosaurs had a wide distribution over the Pangaean continent.

Next time your mom or dad wakes you when you'd rather sleep in, tell them the story of Hans-Dieter Sues. If he hadn't slept in late one morning, the world's oldest Jurassic dinosaurs—200-million-year-old prosauropods—might not have been discovered in Nova Scotia.

Hans-Dieter Sues (see Profile on page 61) travelled to eastern Canada in search of Triassic and Early Jurassic vertebrates (animals with backbones). Much of eastern North America has the right kind of

Famous for its four-storey high tides, the Bay of Fundy in Nova Scotia has cliffs that are a treasure trove of minerals—and of dinosaur fossils. Hans-Dieter Sues even found a bone bed that glittered like treasure when the sun sparkled off bone fragments and fish scales held together with just a little rock. Some dinosaur species are known only from that fish bed.

rocks, but in most places the rocks are overgrown or they have cities built on them. In Nova Scotia, the conditions for dinosaur hunting are better. Hans, along with two colleagues, decided to begin his search in that area.

The Bay of Fundy is famous for the highest tides in the world. By the time Hans was awake, the tide was too high for them to access the rocks from the beach. Rather than waiting several hours for the next low tide, the scientists began crawling along the basalt cliffs to get to the rocks they wanted to look at. It was a drizzly, foggy day and, in the "weird" light, they noticed veins of reddish rock with tiny white specks. The area is rich in minerals, but the specks didn't look like mineral deposits. As they looked more carefully, they saw a little white square. Hans discovered it was a tiny armour plate from an extinct crocodile! By the time the fog had lifted, they had cleared out hundreds of little bone fragments. Hans estimates that there are hundreds of thousands of bones in those deposits.

But where were the 200-million-year-old dinosaurs found? In a nearby rock outcrop formed by ancient sand dunes. The fossil bones and partial skeletons found in this rock layer belong to a group of dinosaurs called prosauropods, herbivores (plant-eaters) with long necks and tails. They grew as long as a camper van and fed on leaves high in trees.

DINO PROFILE

Prosauropod

- Age: 225–190 mya
- Location in Canada: Nova Scotia
- Size: 6.5 m (21 ft) long
- Likely diet: leaves, small twigs of conifer trees, and cycads.
- Special discovery: Prosauropods probably didn't chew their food, but mashed it up in a muscular gizzard full of smooth stones. Scientists occasionally find these stones, called gastroliths, among the bones of prosauropod dinosaurs.
- Current debate: Did the likelihood that prosauropod dinosaurs couldn't chew their food lead to their extinction? Some scientists believe that these dinosaurs were not able to compete with newly evolving species of ornithischian dinosaurs that had flat molars for chewing.

TRACE EVIDENCE

In April 1984, in Parrsboro, Nova Scotia, fossil collector Eldon George uncovered some of the world's smallest dinosaur footprints. The three-toed footprints could fit on a nickel and were made by a creature no bigger than a robin. Other trackways along the Bay of Fundy indicate that many Triassic–Jurassic age dinosaurs were turkey- to ostrich-sized.

ARMOURED DINOSAURS
Living Tanks

Dino Fact

According to Richard McCrea (see Profile on page 68), you wouldn't have to hurry to keep up with an ankylosaur. Richard likens them to slow-moving Cretaceous tanks. Calculations of their top speed, based on trackway evidence, clocks them in at 2 or 3 km (1.2–1.8 miles) per hour.

Close your eyes and try to imagine a living tank. The creature you dream up will probably look a lot like a group of dinosaurs known as ankylosaurs. Except for the bellies, every part of their skins was embedded with bony plates called scutes. Like suits of armour, the location of the scutes gave maximum protection *and* maximum flexibility. So these huge plant-eaters could move somewhat gracefully yet fully protected through the Late Cretaceous landscapes of Alberta.

It's not difficult to recognize the value of all that armour when you consider the size and power of the tyrannosaurid dinosaurs that shared the same environments. In addition to their scutes, some

A NEW PERSPECTIVE

Philip Currie (see Profile on page 39) likes it when palaeontologists from other parts of the globe bring "fresh eyes" to the Alberta badlands. Recently, a Chinese colleague of his discovered an ankylosaur brain case resting on top of a rocky pinnacle in Dinosaur Provincial Park, Alberta. Philip just walked by the pinnacle towards the sandstone layers where fossils are most often found, but his Chinese friend had taken the time to scramble up the pinnacle for a look!

◄ **Only two kinds of armoured dinosaurs have been found in Alberta:** *Euoplocephalus* **(left) and** *Ankylosaurus* **(above), the last, largest, and best-known of the ankylosaurids.**

ankylosaurs had another unique defensive adaptation—a surprisingly large and heavy tail club. Some scientists speculate that ankylosaurs were nimble enough to position their clubs between themselves and a would-be attacker. With a mighty swipe, they may have been able to topple a tyrannosaur, potentially breaking the meat-eater's leg in the process.

Fossils from ankylosaurs are rather rare and only two kinds have been found in Alberta—*Euoplocephalus* and *Ankylosaurus*.

D INO PROFILE

Ankylosaurus

- Age: 74–67 mya
- Location in Canada: Alberta
- Size: 10.6 m (35 ft) long
- Likely diet: plants
- Special discovery: Ankylosaurids are the only group of dinosaurs to have bony tail clubs. In the case of *Ankylosaurus*, the club is as big as a wrecking ball! Surprisingly, trackways of ankylosaurs show no hint of tail drag—these powerful dinosaurs must have held their heavy tails above the ground.
- Current debate: Were ankylosaurs like slow turtles or nimble rhinoceroses? Trackways are helping scientists to try to solve this riddle.

ARMOURED DINOSAURS
Tracking

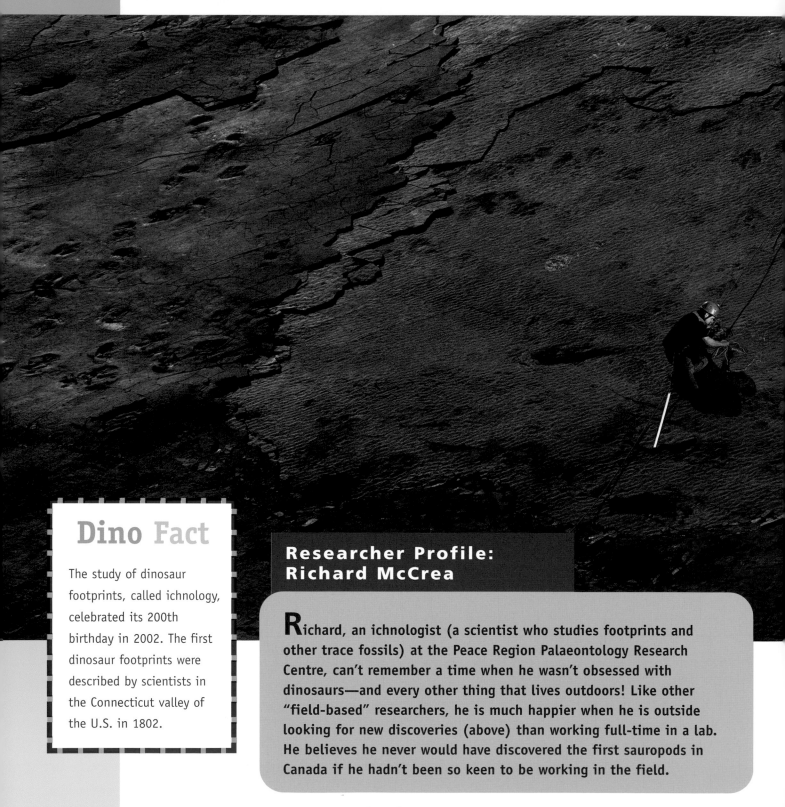

Dino Fact

The study of dinosaur footprints, called ichnology, celebrated its 200th birthday in 2002. The first dinosaur footprints were described by scientists in the Connecticut valley of the U.S. in 1802.

Researcher Profile: Richard McCrea

Richard, an ichnologist (a scientist who studies footprints and other trace fossils) at the Peace Region Palaeontology Research Centre, can't remember a time when he wasn't obsessed with dinosaurs—and every other thing that lives outdoors! Like other "field-based" researchers, he is much happier when he is outside looking for new discoveries (above) than working full-time in a lab. He believes he never would have discovered the first sauropods in Canada if he hadn't been so keen to be working in the field.

Richard McCrea spends a lot of time hanging from climbing ropes on an 18-storey-high cliff in Grande Cache, Alberta. As an ichnologist, Richard was tempted to these great heights by one of the best dinosaur track sites in the world. More than 10,000 footprints spread across the cliff face, providing an extraordinary picture of life in Alberta 100 million years ago. The site is so special, it was recently designated a Provincial Historic Resource, earning it the highest ever level of protection for a fossil trackway. Richard has discovered evidence of a dinosaur community dominated by a herd of armoured dinosaurs called ankylosaurs. Huge meat-eating dinosaurs, several types of theropods (small carnivorous dinosaurs), and heron-like birds all lived together at the Grande Cache location.

How did the dinosaurs get on the steep cliffs? They didn't. What is now a cliff was once an area of flat, soft ground in which muddy footprints filled with sediment. Over time, the entire surface was buried under tremendous pressure and became a rock layer, which was tilted into its current near-vertical position when the Rocky Mountains were formed. A coal miner was the first to discover dinosaur tracks here in 1989. Today, twenty track sites in a 25 km² (10 sq. mi.) area have been found at Grande Cache.

TRACE EVIDENCE

If scientists looked at only bones, they'd know very little about the diversity of dinosaurs that lived in western Canada. The fossil skeletal record only goes back 75 to 80 million years. The footprint record dates from 140 to 135 million years ago! Trace fossils can provide clues that skeletons may not. Like you, every dinosaur created hundreds of thousands of footprints in its life, so even though finding fossilized footprints is rare, it is still much more likely than finding a fossilized skeleton.

WHAT WOULD YOU NAME YOUR FOOTPRINTS?

No one has found a dinosaur dead in its tracks. It's even rare to find dinosaur footprints and fossilized skeletons in the same place. Ichnologists can often determine what type of dinosaur made a footprint—if it was made by a ceratopsian (horned dinosaur), a hadrosaur (duckbill dinosaur), or an ankylosaur (armoured dinosaur). Yet within each of these groups, many species had similar feet, and many foot skeletons are missing.

Because they can't positively link footprints to a dinosaur species, palaeontologists give each kind of dinosaur footprint its own scientific name. Philip Currie (see Profile on page 39) named what turned out to be hadrosaur (duckbill) tracks in Peace River, British Columbia, *Amblydactylus*, "wandering toes!"

The True North

Drive along Calgary's Memorial Drive on a cold, crisp winter day and you'll see something peeking over the highway—a two-storey-high tyrannosaur covered with snow! Impossible for living dinosaurs? Maybe not. Dinosaur bones have been found in the Northwest Territories, in the Yukon, and on the Arctic islands.

The largest number of northern dinosaur bones ever found is scattered along the sides of the Colville River in Alaska: ceratopsian (horned) dinosaurs, a herd of hadrosaur (duckbill) dinosaurs, and teeth from *Albertosaurus* and *Tyrannosaurus*. Plant fossils discovered at the site suggest that the temperature then averaged between 2 and 3 °C (36–37°F)— about the same as the inside of your refrigerator. And there are no fossil lizards, turtles, or amphibians. Then, as now, scientists argue, the north was too chilly for these cold-blooded creatures.

Yet a 1996 discovery on the frigid island of Axel Heiberg in the Canadian Arctic paints a different picture. Scientists discovered fossil bones from an extinct cold-blooded reptile known as a champsosaur. Like all cold-blooded reptiles, champsosaurs relied on the sun to warm their bodies and could not survive freezing temperatures. Don Brinkman (see Profile on page 77)

▲

A 1996 discovery of a champsosaur in the Canadian Arctic suggests that the far north had a drastically different climate 89 million years ago.

Dino Fact

The first dinosaur find in the Canadian Arctic was discovered in 1987 on Bylot Island, near Baffin Island. It was a metatarsal (foot bone) from a young hadrosaur.

and his colleagues concluded that champsosaurs needed an average temperature of at least 14 °C (57°F) to live. The discovery implies that, 89 million years ago, the climate of Axel Heiberg was similar to that of modern-day Florida.

TRACE EVIDENCE

How do scientists know that dinosaurs once roamed central Yukon? They followed their footprints. Roland Gangloff, Curator of Earth Sciences at the University of Alaska Museum in Fairbanks, made this thrilling discovery in 1999 during an after-lunch stroll around the community of Ross River. Roland and his colleague Kevin May later returned to the site to map and measure 200 footprints of several different kinds of dinosaurs.

DINO PROFILE

Leaellynasaura amicagraphica

- Age: 100 mya
- Location: Southeast Australia (100 mya, Australia and Antarctica had not yet drifted apart)
- Size: kangaroo-sized
- Likely diet: plants
- Special discovery: A fossil brain case reveals very large optic lobes—a strong clue that *Leaellynasaura* could see well in the long, dark Antarctic winter.
- Current debate: Did dinosaurs remain in the Antarctic throughout the dark winter months?
  Scientists use the location of fossil finds, as well as trace fossils such as trackways, to determine which dinosaurs may have migrated, and which stayed put.

LIFE IN THE DARK

Warm or cold, dinosaur life in the far north included three or more months of darkness, just as it does today. While fossil footprints suggest that many types of dinosaurs may have migrated south, scientists think that some dinosaur species may have hung out year-round. They point to teeth from a light-boned dinosaur named *Hypsilophodontus* (below), and reason that these dinosaurs were too small to migrate thousands of kilometres. They also point to fossil evidence that big meat-eating dinosaurs overwintered above the Arctic Circle, so prey species had to be present. The North Slope dinosaurs may have survived year-round in ancient long-gone river systems that supported lush summer vegetation. Enough seasonal plant matter may have grown during the 24-hour sunlit summer days to last during the cool-to-cold dark days of winter.

DUCKBILL DINOSAURS
Living in Herds

▲

Known as a "trombone" duckbill, *Parasaurolophus walkeri* sported an elaborate crest. In 1995, a well-preserved *Parasaurolophus* was found in New Mexico, U.S.A. Its enormous crest contained long, looped tubes that led from the nostrils, up to the top of the crest, and then back down towards the throat.

Dino Fact

A hadrosaur thigh-bone was the very first dinosaur bone discovered in western Canada. George Mercer Dawson found the bone near what is today Killdeer, Saskatchewan, when he was serving as naturalist to the British North American Boundary Commission—the survey team responsible for marking the boundary between the United States and Canada.

Which dinosaur family left more fossils than any other? Hadrosaurs, or duckbill dinosaurs. For every theropod skeleton that turns up in Alberta's Dinosaur Provincial Park, there are at least twenty hadrosaurs.

Do all those fossils mean that duckbills were the most common dinosaur in prehistoric Alberta 83 to 65 million years ago? It's impossible to say. The large number of fossil remains may simply mean that hadrosaurs lived in environments where their fossil skeletons were more likely to be preserved.

Witnessing a herd of duckbills would have been a spectacular sight. Scientists have found evidence of herds consisting of hundreds of these giants, 10 to 13 metres (33–43 ft) long, travelling together. Darren Tanke (see Profile on page 31) studies the bones from injured dinosaurs to discover what they can tell him about how dinosaurs lived. Through his examination of more than 5,000 vertebrae from hadrosaur tails, Darren is able to see patterns in duckbill dinosaur life. Young duckbills rarely have broken tails, but by the time they reach adulthood, there's a good chance the tips of their tails will have been crushed, mangled, and fused back together. What's going on? Duckbill dinosaurs lived in large herds. The location, type, and frequency of the breaks suggests to Darren that these large plant-eaters probably trod on one another's tails when they were waking up, drinking from watering holes, or foraging in the forest.

D INO PROFILE

Maiasaura

- Age: 77–73 mya
- Location in Canada: fossilized eggs found in Alberta
- Size: 9 m (29 ft) long
- Likely diet: plants
- Special discovery: A baby *Maiasaura*, fossilized just as it was hatching.
- Current debate: Did *Maiasaura*, "good mother lizard," care for her young? Some scientists use the fact that eggs, adults, and embryos have been found together to support their argument that *Maiasaura* cared for their hatchlings. Evidence from the structure of egg shells, however, suggests that this may not be true.

SOUNDING CRESTS?

Hadrosaurs had a remarkable variety of head crests. Some scientists think the crests were used to generate sounds. In 1995, a well-preserved *Parasaurolophus* was found in New Mexico, U.S.A. Palaeontologists took a CT scan of the long tubes in the 1.5-m (5-ft) long skull. The dinosaur could have made resonating sounds in its crest, just as you can produce noises by blowing across the top of a bottle. The sound would have been quite low, similar in pitch to the lowest note on a piano. Scientists believe that these hadrosaur calls would have travelled well through the dense vegetation in which they lived. The vocalizations could have been used to coordinate group movement or even as alarm calls.

Some scientists believe that male, female, and juvenile hadrosaurs may have had different sizes and shapes of crests, and that these were visual cues for identifying mates. Note that the crests of the *Lambeosaurus lambei* (top) and the *Corythosaurus casuarivus* (bottom) not only differ in size and shape, but in how much space there is in the holes of the skull.

DUCKBILL DINOSAURS
Life in the Nest

▲

From this reconstruction of a hadrosaur embryo, we can see that hadrosaurs were hatched from round, or spherical, eggs.

Dino Fact

Dinosaur egg fragments are extremely rare in Canada outside of Devil's Coulee, Alberta. Fewer than 200 bits of shell have been found in Dinosaur Provincial Park, and only four tiny pieces in all of Saskatchewan. With an estimated 2,000,000 eggs in 1,000 km² (386 sq. mi.), the Xixia Basin, in Henan Province, China, is one of the premier sites for dinosaur eggs in the world.

Take an egg out of the refrigerator and have a good close look. Darla Zelenitsky classifies the similarities and differences between eggs, but the ones she examines don't come from refrigerators, or even chickens—they come from dinosaurs!

It's hard to imagine how something as breakable as an egg could ever be fossilized. But in the past ten years, a number of exciting discoveries of fossilized eggs and nests have been made in Mongolia, China, South America, and Canada. Darla uses distinct characteristics, such as texture, of even tiny fossilized eggshell fragments to help her determine what kind of animal laid it. Working in Devil's Coulee, Alberta,

Darla has identified ten different types of eggs from the site—crocodile, turtle, bird, and various kinds of duckbill and theropod dinosaurs.

She cuts thin sections of dinosaur eggshells and examines them under high magnification. She compares their structure to eggshells from living animals, such as ostriches, turtles, and crocodiles. Animals that bury their eggs have shells that are quite porous. Water vapour travels more easily through these eggs than through birds' eggs, which are less porous.

Shells of hadrosaur (duckbill) dinosaur eggs are similar to those of turtles and crocodiles in some ways—strong evidence that mother duckbills probably buried their eggs and left. The structure of the eggs of theropods (small meat-eating dinosaurs), however, were much like those of birds, and Darla suspects that these dinosaurs incubated their eggs on a nest. Discoveries in Mongolia of a number of specimens of *Oviraptor* (a small theropod) sitting on a clutch of eggs adds even more strength to this theory, as do other finds of *Oviraptor* with eggs containing embryos.

The discovery of fossilized embryos with eggs helps palaeontologists identify which dinosaurs laid which eggs. This then can help Darla identify eggshell fragments. Like dinosaur footprints, every species of dinosaur egg has its own unique name. The elongated eggs from the dinosaur *Oviraptor*, for instance, are called *Elongatoolithus*. Round, spherical eggs from a hadrosaur at Devil's Coulee are *Spheroolithus*.

Both the partially excavated theropod egg clutch (bottom) and the fossilized eggs (top)—probably from a lambeosaur—were found in Montana. There is evidence that the theropod eggs were kept warm and hatched by a parent dinosaur, just as bird eggs are today.

Researcher Profile: Darla Zelenitsky

Darla, a researcher at the University of Calgary, grew up in Manitoba where there are no dinosaurs. Today, she is one of only about four people in the whole world who specialize in dinosaur eggs. Her love of dinosaurs began at the age of four, when her parents used to read her dinosaur books.

Where Have All the Dinosaurs Gone?

▲

We know the extinction of the dinosaurs happened 65 million years ago, but there are several theories as to why. Here's one: a second before impact, a comet passes through Earth's atmosphere. About 10 seconds after impact, a plume of vaporized rock and water rises 100 kilometres (62 miles) through the atmosphere. Within about 20 minutes, the shock wave will kill the saurolophine hadrosaurs in the foreground.

Many species evolved and became extinct through the 160-million-year-long age of the dinosaurs. But 65 million years ago, at the end of the Cretaceous, 50 to 75 percent of all species became extinct during the Cretaceous/Tertiary mass extinction, called the K-T extinction (to distinguish it from the smaller Cenomanian-Turonian extinction 94 million years ago). What happened?

Three major events are being investigated:

Ka-boom!

In 1980, scientists put forth the idea that a giant asteroid hit the Earth, supported by high levels of the rare Earth element iridium in rocks formed at the time of the final dinosaur extinction (which scientists call the "K-T boundary"). Some scientists suspect that the impact sent tremendous amounts of dust into the atmosphere where it could have blocked the sun, forming acid rain, preventing plants from photosynthesizing (converting sunlight into energy), and creating sub-freezing temperatures for months or years.

Blast Off!

Other scientists focus on the volcanic activity occurring worldwide in the millions of years leading up to the K-T boundary. Unlike an asteroid impact with effects felt within days or years, ongoing volcanic eruptions would have spewed lava and rock particles into the atmosphere sporadically over time. The long-term effect would have been global cooling over millions of years.

Changing Habitats

In the last few million years of the Cretaceous, the vast, shallow inland seas that once covered much of the Prairie provinces receded, causing a drastic reduction in the coastal plains where dinosaurs lived.

Many palaeontologists believe it was a combination of these physical events that likely caused the eventual extinction of the dinosaurs.

BUILT TO LAST

Press your nose against the glass of a terrarium and have a good, close look at the turtles and amphibians inside. Believe it or not, you are looking at animals that are little changed from their 75-million-year-old relatives. How did so many types of turtles, frogs, and salamanders cross the K-T boundary? According to Don Brinkman, small animals had a lot better chance of finding refuges where they could survive the effects of a meteor impact than their big dinosaur neighbours.

Researcher Profile: Don Brinkman

Don was so enthusiastic about fossils when he was a kid that he planned on becoming a geologist. He discovered a program at the University of Edmonton that combined geology with biology. Don loves the excitement of discovery, whether it's finding something new in the field or explaining relationships between climate and turtle diversity. Today he is Head of Research and Curator of Vertebrate Palaeontology at the Royal Tyrrell Museum of Palaeontology.

INTO THE FUTURE

Our understanding of dinosaurs and other prehistoric animals is constantly changing. At one time, pterodactyls were thought to have been incapable of flying. It was believed that these winged reptiles could do little more than hug the sides of cliffs hoping for a wind strong enough to move them. Recent evidence, however, suggests that pterodactyls were quite good flyers and that they flew with their hind limbs tucked up under their bodies like birds. Similarly, the once "solitary" *Tyrannosaurus rex* now appears to have lived in social groups, at least for part of its life.

Ideas about how dinosaurs moved and behaved are also changing. Look in an older dinosaur book and you'll read that sauropods were too heavy to support their own weight, having to stick to swamps to keep from collapsing. Yet, with modern technology, it now appears that sauropod limbs were about as strong as those of elephants—certainly strong enough to support their own body weight on land. In fact, the hind limbs of sauropods were much stronger than their forelimbs, leading some scientists to speculate that sauropods may have stood up on their back legs to reach higher leaves and twigs. Other scientists dispute the idea, claiming that such a posture would have raised the sauropods' heads too far above their hearts. Recent analysis suggests that, if this were true, the blood pressure of a sauropod would have been twice that of a giraffe—the animal with the highest blood pressure of any living creature. How did sauropods cope with high blood pressure? No one yet knows. But when a researcher does solve this riddle, it will be just one more piece in the complex puzzle that makes up our understanding of dinosaurs.

Did these sauropods suffer from high blood pressure? In the future, we may find the answer.

Bringing Dinosaurs to Life

Dino Fact

Donna Sloan is working in a tradition that is much older than photography as a way to capture fossil images. The first illustration of a dinosaur bone was drawn in 1677.

Donna Sloan toyed with a real turtle to see exactly how, 70 million years ago, a Boremys turtle would have reacted to the curiosity of a *Troodon*.

The task of breathing life into the bones and trace material that make up the fossil record falls to talented dinosaur illustrators and model makers. Once they focused primarily on how dinosaurs might have looked, but they now have the even more challenging task of portraying how dinosaurs might have lived.

Donna Sloan, a dinosaur illustrator at the Royal Tyrrell Museum, is working on an illustration of a *Troodon*. This human-sized theropod (meat-eater) is believed to have been the smartest dinosaur, because it had the largest brain in proportion to its body weight. Donna wonders how a smart dinosaur might use its grasping hands on one of the turtles that shared its Alberta habitat 70 million years ago. And how would the turtle have reacted? Donna heads for the palaeoconservatory to find out. She finds that if she picks up a turtle, it tucks in all of its legs; if she lifts the back end, its front legs pop out; if she lifts the front end, the back legs and tail come out. She hurries back to her drawing table.

When she isn't observing live animals, Donna studies skeletons, both recent and fossilized. The shape and structure of bones, and the placement of muscle scar marks, help her understand how an animal might have moved or held a certain posture. Using this knowledge, Donna helps palaeontologists breathe life into fossilized specimens.

Donna enjoys it when a scientist gives her a few bones and asks her to "draw the animal." With just a jaw, a vertebra (a piece of backbone), a couple of scutes (bony plates), and part of a skull roof, Donna worked to recreate what one scientist described as a "croc-like" animal. In the library, she looked up information on the animal's known relatives. She could tell from the vertebra that the mystery animal probably lived in the sea (land animals support their own weight, so their vertebrae are usually more robust). Donna measured the vertebra to estimate the animal's size.

The jaw and skull piece provided their own set of riddles. The jaw was like a tyrannosaur's, but the skull was flat like a crocodile's. Back to the library, to read how different shapes of jaws and teeth affect ways of eating. Donna reasoned that the animal yanked its prey, as a crocodile does. So instead of flippers, it might have had legs to brace itself. The scutes, which help support an animal's body, also suggested that the animal might have crawled onto land. So legs it was. By taking tiny clues and tracking down as much information as possible, Donna created an image of the mystery animal.

Recently Donna created a series of paper silhouettes to enable a scientist to study how a specific bone in a tyrannosaur's foot moved as the dinosaur ran forward.

▼

When Donna is given a more complete skeleton, she spends her time measuring and carefully examining each bone. Often, she'll stop in the middle of an illustration to build a wire sculpture or clay model of the dinosaur to give her a better idea of its shape and posture. She'll do gesture drawings to figure out if a real animal could actually move in the way she has depicted it. And she'll draw side, top, and bottom views of the same bone to get a 360-degree perspective. Back and forth, back and forth, she compares her knowledge of muscles of modern-day birds and crocodiles with clues found on the fossilized bones.

Over time and with much experience, Donna's work has become bolder. Instead of focusing only on dinosaur anatomy, she portrays behaviour, creating a charging *Gorgosaurus* or her *Troodon* grabbing a turtle. Her commitment to recreating life extends to prehistoric environments. On a holiday to Florida, Donna took countless rolls of pictures of bald cypress (a common tree in Late Cretaceous Alberta) and spent hours sketching the different gestures these plants make. She has an entire collection of photos of leaf litter, many showing tiny cones and plant fronds, so that she can add these details to her pictures of small prehistoric mammals. Donna constantly thinks of the next dinosaur picture she wants to create. With new species being discovered each year, there is no end to the rich prehistoric world she loves to portray.

Whether it's a reconstruction of a new species of ichthyosaur found in British Columbia (left), or a breathtaking image of a *T. rex* wandering off into the Cretaceous landscape of 83–65 million years ago (below), Donna Sloan's images bring long-extinct creatures to life before our eyes.

DONNA'S TIPS FOR HOW TO DRAW A DINOSAUR

- Start by drawing something you really enjoy watching. Donna got her start drawing local birds.
- Look for details. What colours and marks do you see?
- When you're ready to try a dinosaur, begin by looking at the skeleton (in a book or at a museum).
- Measure each bone. Look carefully at its shape, and sketch exactly what you see.
- Set a goal of drawing the best picture you can. Ask yourself, "why doesn't this look right?" Find out more about the skeleton to help you improve each drawing.

Researcher Profile: Donna Sloan

Donna loved imagining what dinosaurs looked like when she was a girl. Like Philip Currie, she remembers reading Roy Chapman Andrew's books about digging for dinosaurs in Mongolia and, as she read, she made mental pictures of the scenes written on each page. She was already a wildlife artist when she heard that the soon-to-be-built Tyrrell Museum was looking for volunteers to collect fossils for their new galleries. She signed up and later took a job in one of the palaeontology labs, preparing specimens, moulds, casts, and mounts for display. Today, Donna works as a dinosaur artist at the Royal Tyrrell Museum of Palaeontology.

NEW DISCOVERIES AWAIT

Dinosaurs were around for a long time, but that doesn't mean that everything to know about them has been determined. After all, there are nearly 10,000 species of birds and 4,000 species of mammals alive today. Contrast those numbers to the 500 species of dinosaurs that have been identified, and consider the 160-million-year reign of the dinosaurs. A number of scientists believe that less than 1 percent of all dinosaurs have been discovered. Each new discovery will spark new questions to investigate.

If you could peek inside Philip Currie's passport, you'd find stamps from China, Argentina, the United States, and dozens of other countries. Canadian palaeontologists often travel the world, working with international colleagues to uncover new ideas about dinosaurs. In 2004, Phil and colleagues in the U.S. teamed up to study dinosaur growth. They discovered that *T. rex* had a monstrous growth spurt between the ages of 14 and 18 years—growing from a 1-ton carnivore to a 6-ton dinosaur-eating machine. During those four years a *T. rex* gained as much as 2 kg (4 ½ lbs) each day.

Canada is so dinosaur rich, you might even discover a dinosaur while walking your dog. That's exactly how a fellow found an *Edmontosaurus* (duckbill dinosaur) right in the city of Edmonton, Alberta. Excavations began on the site in 2006. Already palaeontologists have unearthed a group of *Edmontosaurus* and a couple of tyrannosaurs, most likely *Albertosaurus* and *Daspletosaurus*. Right now, researchers are preparing fossil *Pachyrhinosaurus* (horned dinosaurs) from the Pipestone Creek Bonebed site near the city of Grande Prairie in Alberta. The bonebed contains up to 100 bones per square metre. So far 3,500 bones, including 14 skulls have been removed, making it the second-largest dinosaur site in North America.

When many of the researchers in this book were kids, there were only a few jobs in palaeontology. Happily, that's changing with lots of new discoveries awaiting and exciting, new ways of looking at dinosaurs.

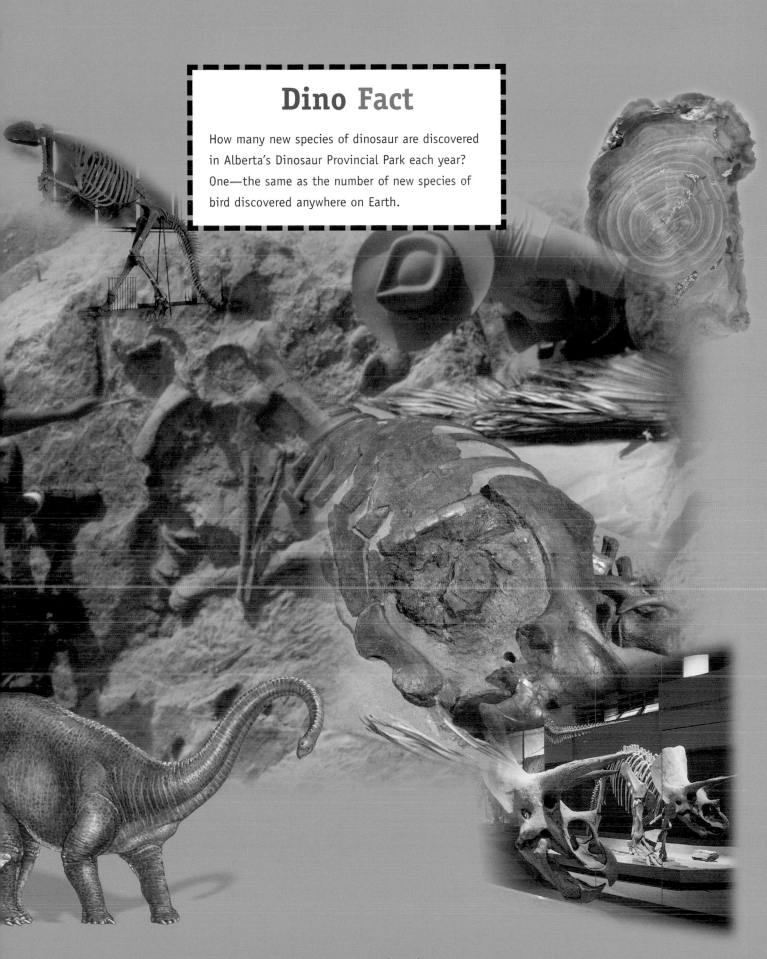

Dino Fact

How many new species of dinosaur are discovered in Alberta's Dinosaur Provincial Park each year? One—the same as the number of new species of bird discovered anywhere on Earth.

Dinosaurs in Canada

Putting together a complete list of dinosaurs found in Canada is tricky. The list continues to change as new species are found and identified, and as new information changes the way dinosaurs are categorized and named. As you look through the list, you'll notice that in some places, such as Alberta, palaeontologists know a lot of specific information about which dinosaurs lived during different time periods. In other places, fossil bones are too fragmented to be identified. This list also includes some trackways—another essential source of information about Canadian dinosaurs.

Yukon Territory
Bones (90–65 mya)
Hadrosaur (a tail vertebra and a few fragments of a finger)

Trackways (100 mya)
Saurischian:
Ornithomimipus
Irenesauripus
Gypsichnites

Ornithischian:
Amblydactylus cf. kortmeyeri
Amblydactylus sp.
Hadrosaurichnus
Iguanodontipus
Tetrapodosaurus (armoured dinosaur form)
Indeterminate prints of a four-toed ornithischian

Northwest Territories
Bones (65–70 mya)
Ceratopsian (fragments of frill and skull)

Nunavut
Bones (~70 mya)
Hadrosaur (fragments of jaw and foot)

British Columbia
Bones (98–65 mya)
Theropod

Trackways (125 mya)
More than 1,700 tracks in more than 100 trackways. These trackways contained:
• 60% hadrosaur trackways (hand and footprints)
• At least 4 species of carnivorous dinosaurs (10% large, 20% medium and small)
• Ceratopsian
• Iguanodon
• Primitive ankylosaur

Trackways (97–95 mya)
Tetrapodosaurus (armoured dinosaur form)
News Flash! Palaeontologists are currently excavating unidentified bones from a plant-eating dinosaur found in the same location as these tracks!

Trackways (Age to be determined)
News Flash! See page 63 for information on the discovery of the first sauropod footprints in Canada

Special note: Thanks to the newly created Peace River Palaeontology Research Centre, B.C. now has two resident vertebrate palaeontologists. They are excavating so many bones from the Tumbler Ridge area, and responding to calls from people finding dinosaur trackways in the southeast and other parts of the province, the information about what dinosaurs once lived in B.C. is changing FAST! See www.tumblerridgemuseum.com and www.canadatracks.com/ for the most complete listings.

Alberta
Theropods (78 mya)
Aublysodon sp.
Daspletosaurus torosus
Dromaeosaurus sp.
Gorgosaurus sp.
Ornithomimidae
Paronychodon sp.
Richardoestesia sp.
Saurornitholestes sp.
Troodon sp.

Hypsilophodonts (78 mya)
Orodromeus makelai

Pachycephalosaurs (78 mya)
Stegoceras validum

Hadrosaurs (78 mya)
Hypacrosaurus stebingeri
Lambeosaurinae

Ankylosaurs (78 mya)
Euoplocephalus
Nodosauridae

Ceratopsians (78 mya)
Centrosaurus
Chasmosaurinae
Montanoceratops cerorhynchus

Theropods (76.5–74.5 mya)
Aublysodon sp.
Avimimus sp.
Chirostenotes collinsi
Chirostenotes sternbergi
Daspletosaurus
Dromaeosaurus albertensis
Dromiceiomimus samueli
Elmisaurus elegans
Erlikosaurus sp.

Gorgosaurus libratus
Ornithomimus edmontonensis
Richardoestesia gilmorei
Saurornitholestes langstoni
Struthiomimus altus
Troodon formosus

Hypsilophodontids (76.5–74.5 mya)
Hypsilophodontidae

Hadrosaurs (76.5–74.5 mya)
Brachylophosaurus canadensis
Corythosaurus casuarius
Gryposaurus notabilis
Kritosaurus incurvimanus
Lambeosaurus lambei
Lambeosaurus magnicristatus
Parasaurolophus walkeri
Prosaurolophus maximus

Ankylosaurs (76.5–74.5 mya)
Edmontonia longiceps
Euoplocephalus tutus
Panoplosaurus mirus
Pachycephalosauridae
Gravitholus albertae
Ornatotholus browni
Pachycephalosaurus sp.
Stegoceras validum
Undescribed full-domed pachycephalosaurid

Ceratopsians (76.5–74.5 mya)
Anchiceratops sp.
Centrosaurus apertus
Centrosaurus nasicornus
Chasmosaurus irvinensis
Chasmosaurus belli
Chasmosaurus russelli
Leptoceratops sp.
Styracosaurus albertensis

Theropods (70 mya)
Albertosaurus sarcophagus
Aublysodon sp.
Chirostenotes pergracilis
Daspletosaurus
Dromaeosaurus sp.
Dromiceiomimus brevitertius
Ornithomimus edmontonticus
Struthiomimus altus
Troodon sp.
Velociraptorinae

Hypsilophodonts (70 mya)
Parksosaurus warreni

Pachycephalosaurs (70 mya)
Stegoceras edmontonense

Hadrosaurs (70 mya)
Edmontosaurus regalis
Hypacrosaurus altispinus
Saurolophus osborni

Ankylosaurs (70 mya)
Edmontonia longiceps

Euoplocephalus tutus
Panoplosaurus sp.

Ceratopsians (70 mya)
Anchiceratops ornatus
Arrhinoceratops brachyops
Pachyrhinosaurus canadensis

Two famous Canadian dinosaurs, *Tyrannosaurus rex* and *Triceratops,* did not show up in the Alberta fossil record until very near the end of the Age of Dinosaurs, approximately 67–65 million years ago. Dinosaur trackways have also been found in Alberta. Look to page 68 for a recent discovery!

Saskatchewan
(many of these dinosaurs are also found in the same age rocks in Alberta)
Theropods (65 mya)
Tyrannosaurus rex
Dromaeosaurus sp.
Troodon sp.
Sauronitholestes sp.
Richardoestesia sp.
Ornithomimidae

Hadrosaurs (65 mya)
Edmontosaurus saskatchewanensis

Ankylosaurs (65 mya)
Ankylosauria

Pachycephalosaurs (65 mya)
Pachycephalosauridae

Ceratopsians (65 mya)
Triceratops horridus
Torosaurus sp.

Manitoba
No dinosaurs found here (but there were incredible prehistoric marine reptiles such as mosasaurs and plesiosaurs).

Ontario, Quebec, New Brunswick, Prince Edward Island, Newfoundland and Labrador
No dinosaurs found here.

Nova Scotia
Bones (225–205 mya)
unidentified ornithischian
unidentified prosauropod

Trackways (225–205 mya)
Atreipus (an ornithischian)
Grallator (a ceratosaurian theropod)

Bones (205–180 mya)
Ammosaurus (a prosauropod)
Anchisaurus (a prosauropod)
Undescribed primitive ornithiscian

Trackways (205–180 mya)
Grallator
Eubrontes (a theropod)
Anomoepus (an ornithischian)

Dinosaur Time

Grasping time isn't always easy. Just imagine how difficult it is to fathom the incredible length of time that dinosaurs lived on Earth, and how much time has passed since then. Scientists use an instrument called the geological time scale to measure the history and ages of the Earth in an understandable way. That history stretches back about 4.5 billion years ago to the time when the Earth was formed. The time scale breaks time down into smaller, more manageable chunks, called eras. The Mesozoic Era spans an astonishing 160 million years and can be further divided into three main periods: The Triassic, the Jurassic, and the Cretaceous. It's impossible to describe the inconceivable diversity of environments, plants, and animals that evolved and disappeared during this 160-million-year-old time frame. The following is just a taste of what the Earth looked like during each of those periods and the major groups of dinosaurs that lived during those times.

The Triassic Period
(225–200 million years ago)

The Jurassic Period
(200–135 million years ago)

The Cretaceous Period
(135–65 million years ago)

If you could travel back in time to the Triassic Period and look down on Earth, you wouldn't be able to recognize it. All of the continents that we know today were fused together to form a gigantic land area named Pangaea ("all Earth"). The continent was so large, much of the interior was a long distance from the sea. As a result, climates were very hot and dry. It was extremely difficult for animals to survive in these climates and few species existed. The first remains of dinosaurs were found in rocks dating back to about 225 million years ago. The rocks that now form the cliffs of the Bay of Fundy were home to some of these earliest dinosaurs—prosauropods, early ornithiscian dinosaurs—and numerous trackways of various kinds of predatory dinosaurs. You can read more about these dinosaurs on pages 64–65.

During the Jurassic Period, the supercontinent Pangaea was beginning to shift and, eventually, to break up. Narrow seaways spread between the future continents, resulting in milder, wetter climates. These milder climates supported a greater diversity and abundance of plants. The largest and most amazing-looking dinosaurs—the sauropods—lived during the Jurassic Period. With some individual specimens growing to lengths of more than 50 metres (165 feet) and weighing 100 tons, these dinosaurs were extraordinary plant-processing factories. Turn to page 63 to explore what may prove to be a groundbreaking discovery of sauropod footprints in Canada!

The Cretaceous world first seemed little different from Jurassic times. But as the Cretaceous unfolded, a fascinating variety of dinosaurs evolved. The supercontinent of Pangaea broke into a northern continent (Laurasia) and a southern continent (Gondwana). Over millions and millions of years, these large continents divided and shifted, joined and separated, eventually resulting in an arrangement of continents that looked quite like the world we know today. All this shifting and changing resulted in a rich variety of climates and habitats, and thus an extraordinary diversity of new plant and animal species.

New and diverse groups of herbivorous (plant-eating) dinosaurs, such as the pachycephalosaurs, the ceratopsians, and ornithopods appeared. *Iguanodon*, one of the best known ornithopods, ranged across the northern continents during the Early Cretaceous times. New types of carnivorous (meat-eating) dinosaurs also lived at this time. These included oviraptorosaurs, therizinosaurs, and spinosaurs.

A huge variety of herbivorous and carnivorous dinosaurs called the Late Cretaceous home. You would have seen the wonderful crests and horns of ceratopsians, the oddly shaped crests of hadrosaursian or duckbill dinosaurs, and the horrifying teeth of large tyrannosaurs.

Sixty-five million years ago, the world of dinosaurs ended. The only survivors were the specialized feathered dinosaurs that we call birds today. Turn to pages 76–77 to read more about extinction theories.

Glossary

Ankylosaurs
A group of armoured, plant-eating dinosaurs that lived from the mid-Jurassic to the late Cretaceous periods.

Archosaurs
A major group of reptiles including the dinosaurs, pterosaurs, thecodontians—all of which are extinct—and the living crocodiles.

Badlands
A dry, barren region characterized by wonderfully shaped eroded rocks, as found in parts of southern Saskatchewan and Alberta. Nickamed "badlands" because they were thought to be of little use for anything, they are, instead, treasure troves for fossils.

Bone bed
A collection of fossil bones from one location.

Carnivores
Meat-eaters

Ceratopsians
Commonly known as "horned dinosaurs," these large, Cretaceous, plant-eaters had distinctive horns and head frills.

Champsosaurs
Lizard-like reptiles that lived in water and are now extinct.

Dromaeosaurs
A family of small, fast, Cretaceous, meat-eaters with large, retractable toe claws, and big eyes. They are believed to have been among the smartest dinosaurs.

Fossils
The remains or traces of plants or animals that lived in the past.

Geology
The scientific study of the origin, history, and structure of the Earth's crust.

Hadrosaurs
A large and common group of Late Cretaceous, plant-eating dinosaurs that are often referred to as duckbills because of their distinctive, bill-shaped snouts.

Herbivores
Plant-eaters

Histology
The scientific study of the structures of animal and plant tissues as seen through a microscope.

Holotype
The first specimen of a species to be scientifically described. Also known as a type specimen.

Ichnology
The science of studying dinosaur footprints and other trace fossils.

K-T Extinction
The mass extinction that marked the end of the Cretaceous period, about 65 million years ago.

Meteor
A mass of interplanetary rock or dust particles that creates a streak of light in the night sky when it enters the Earth's atmosphere.

Ornithischian

One of the two major groups of dinosaurs based on hip structure. All ornithischians are plant-eaters. The group includes ceratopsians, ankylosaurs, stegosaurs, pachycephalosaurs, and ornithopods.

Ornithomimids

These ostrich-like, meat-eating dinosaurs had toothless beaks, long legs, and lightweight skeletons.

Outcrop

A rock that protrudes above the surface of the soil.

Palaeobotany

The study of ancient plants.

Palaeoecology

The scientific study of the relation of ancient living organisms to their environment.

Palaeontology

The study of ancient life.

Palynology

The study of spores and pollen.

Pangaea

The enormous super-continent, which characterized the Earth's surface 200 million years ago.

Plaster jacket

The protective covering of plaster and burlap that is wrapped around fragile dinosaur bone during excavation.

Pterodactyls

A sub-group of pterosaurs—flying, prehistoric reptiles.

Quarry

A dinosaur dig site.

Saurischian

One of the two major groups of dinosaurs based on hip structure. The group includes the meat-eating theropods and plant-eating sauropodomorphs.

Sauropods

A group of giant, plant-eating dinosaurs with extremely long necks and whip-tails.

Sediment

Material, like rock and sand, deposited by wind or water.

Sedimentary rock

Rock that has formed from sediment. Most fossils are found in exposed sedimentary rock.

Theropods

A broad group of meat-eating dinosaurs that moved on powerful back legs and were related to modern-day birds.

Trace fossils

Unlike body fossils, which are the remains of dead bodies, trace fossils record the active movements and behaviours of ancient animals. Besides footprints, trace fossils include fossilized burrows, dens, feeding tunnels, eggs, nests, stomach contents, coprolites (poop), tooth and claw marks, and any other product or trace formed while an animal was still alive. The study of trace fossils is known as ichnology.

Tyrannosaurs

A family of large, meat-eating, Late Cretaceous dinosaurs.

Dinosaur Institutions

Here are some of the major dinosaur and fossil destinations in Canada.

British Columbia
Yoho National Park/Parks Canada
Field, British Columbia
www.parkscanada.ca/
A UNESCO World Heritage Site. Vistors can touch Burgess Shale fossil specimens and learn about mountain building, rock types, geological processes, and geological time.

Tumbler Ridge Museum and Dinosaur Centre
Tumbler Ridge, British Columbia
www.tumblerridgemuseum.com
When the Tumbler Ridge boys (see page 16) made their spectacular discovery, they set off a wave of enthusiasm for palaeontology in their community. The result: a brand new museum and research centre that offers dinosaur camps for kids, special lectures, and exhibits.

Alberta
The Calgary Zoo's Prehistoric Park
Calgary, Alberta
www.calgaryzoo.ab.ca
The Calgary Zoo's Prehistoric Park is unique to the world. Enter the park and travel into a recreation of western Canada as it might have appeared when dinosaurs reigned supreme. More than 100 species of plants and a collection of life-sized dinosaurs reflect our present understanding of that ancient time.

Devil's Coulee Dinosaur Heritage Museum
Warner, Alberta
www.devilscoulee.com
Home to a large variety of palaeontological displays, many of which are hands-on. Visitors can tour the first dinosaur nesting site (duckbill dinosaurs) discovered in Canada.

Dinosaur Provincial Park
Patricia, Alberta
www.cd.gov.ab.ca/parks/dinosaur
Explore one of the world's most significant fossil beds set in the spectacular badlands. This UNESCO World Heritage Site offers an experience of a lifetime. Most of the park is a restricted natural preserve and access is only through interpretive bus tours and guided hikes. Watch fossil preparation and view the exhibits at the Field Station Visitor Centre.

River of Death and Discovery Dinosaur Centre
www.riverofdeath.ca
This proposed new facility currently exists as a virtual museum. It details a mass death site for *Pachyrhinosaurus* near Grande Prairie, Alberta. It has extreme significance because of the density of disarticulated skeletons found there—more than 3,500 bones!

The Royal Tyrrell Museum of Palaeontology
Drumheller, Alberta
www.tyrrellmuseum.com
The Royal Tyrrell Museum is devoted exclusively to studying and exhibiting ancient life through fossils. You can explore fascinating displays of dinosaurs and other ancient life, take part in interpretive programming, and catch exciting glimpses into current palaeontological research. You can also help dig up dinosaurs on exciting hands-on excavation tours.

Saskatchewan
Royal Saskatchewan Museum
Regina, Saskatchewan
www.royalsaskmuseum.ca
An Earth Sciences Gallery depicts 2 billion years of geological history. Hands-on learning about fossils is encouraged in the Palaeo Pit.

T. rex Discovery Centre
Eastend, Saskatchewan
www.dinocountry.com
Vistors can watch palaeontologists work on fossils collected from the Frenchman River Valley. Exhibits, educational activities, summer programs, and guided quarry tours are all available.

Manitoba
Canadian Fossil Discovery Centre
Morden, Manitoba
www.discoverfossils.com
The Morden Museum houses Canada's largest collection of Cretaceous marine vertebrates—the amazing aquatic reptiles that ruled Earth's oceans during the last days of the dinosaurs. The museum offers life-size displays of 80-million-year-old mosasaurs and plesiosaurs, as well as ancient birds, sea turtles, fish (including sharks), and even giant squid. Join a "Palaeo Tour" or attend "Palaeo School."

Ontario
Canadian Museum of Nature
Ottawa, Ontario
www.nature.ca/nature_e.cfm
All of the Canadian Museum of Nature's dinosaur skeletons date from the final period of dinosaur life on Earth, the Late Cretaceous Period of 90 to 65 million years ago. Visitors see real fossilized bones, with some pieces modelled from plaster or fibreglass, in the many skeletons on display. All Canadian finds, these dinosaurs would have roamed territory that is now the Prairies and the northern United States.

Royal Ontario Museum
Toronto, Ontario
www.rom.on.ca/
Dinosaurs roam the ROM in the Dinosaur Gallery, located on the Life Sciences floor. Set in vivid diorama surroundings, complete skeletons bring to life some of the large animals of the Jurassic and Cretaceous periods. These walk-through dioramas are complemented by video stations commenting on dinosaur types, skeletal structures, habitats, and ways of life. A small theatre tells the story of fossil-hunting in the badlands of Alberta—one of the richest dinosaur collecting areas in the world.

Quebec
Parc de Miguasha
Nouvelle, Quebec
www.sepaq.com
Dinosaurs in Quebec? Palaeontologists have not yet discovered any traces of dinosaurs in Quebec, but if you're interested in older fossils, Parc de Miguasha protects unique upper Devonian formations, which are of international interest. The park also has a museum of Natural History with exhibits, research facilities, and a library.

Nova Scotia
Fundy Geological Museum
Parrsboro, Nova Scotia
www.museum.gov.ns.ca/fgm/
Visitors are able to see 200-million-year-old dinosaurs, and the incredible mineral specimens in the museum's galleries.

Photo & Illustration Credits

Care has been taken to trace ownership of copyright materials contained in this book. Information enabling the publisher to rectify any reference or credit line in future editions will be welcomed.

RTMP, AB = Royal Tyrrell Museum of Palaeontology, Alberta
CMN = Canadian Museum of Nature
NHMPL= Natural History Museum Picture Library

page 1: by Christopher Srnka; 5 (top): De Agostini/NHMPL; 5 (middle): by Christopher Srnka; 5 (bottom): by Mark Hallett/Mark Hallet Paleoart; 6 (top): by Joe Tucciarone; 6 (bottom): Jenny Halstead/NHMPL; 8: courtesy Calgary Zoo, AB/Prehistoric Park; 9: Vivien Bowers; 10: Corythosaurus by Eleanor Kish reproduced with permission of CMN, Ottawa, Canada; 11-13: with permission of RTMP, AB; 14 (main): Kevin Morris/Lone Pine Photo; 14 (inset): Vince Streano/CORBIS/MAGMA; 15: John L. Bykerk/Lone Pine Photo; 16, 17 (middle): courtesy Dr. Charles Helm; 17 (top): De Agostini/NHMPL; 17 (bottom): with permission of the Minister of Public Works & Government Services Canada, 2003/courtesy of Natural Resources of Canada, Geological Survey of Canada; 18: Glenbow Archives NA-3250-8; 19: Ewell Sale Stewart Library, The Academy of Natural Sciences of Philadelphia; 20: reproduced with permission of CMN, Ottawa, Canada; 21 (top): 19508/American Museum of Natural History Library; 21 (bottom): reproduced with permission of the Minister of Public Works & Government Services, Canada, 2003/courtesy of Natural Resources of Canada, Geological Survery of Canada; 22: Glenbow Archives NA-3250-10; 23: 18547/American Museum of Natural History Library; 24: with permission of Darren Tanke; 25: Dan Splaine/JASON Foundation for Education; 26: reproduced with permission of the Toronto Public Library; 27: with permission of Darren Tanke; 28: Richard Martin, with permission of CMN, Ottawa, Canada; 29 (top): Royce Hopkins/Lone Pine Photo; 29 (bottom): N.C. Museum of Natural Sciences; 30 (excluding camera): with permission of RTMP, AB; 30 (bottom right): courtesy of Canon Canada Inc.; 31(top): with permission of RTMP, AB; 31 (middle): courtesy of Prairie Geomatics Ltd.; 31 (bottom): with permission of Darren Tanke; 32-33 (main): Ex Terra Foundation with permission of RTMP, AB; 33 (inset): by Christopher Srnka; 35; Triceratops by Eleanor Kish reproduced with permission of CMN, Ottawa, Canada; 36: by Jim Zuckerman; 37: with permission of RTMP, AB; 38: The 'Modern' Cretaceous by Eleanor Kish reproduced with permission of CMN, Ottawa, Canada; 39 : with permission of RTMP, AB; 40: Robert Clark/Aurora; 41 (left): Clarence W. Norris/Lone Pine Photo; 41 (right): Karen Chin; 42-43: Royal Saskatchewan Museum; 44: by Mark Hallett/Mark Hallett Paleoart; 45 (top): Clarence W. Norris/Lone Pine Photo; 45 (bottom): Ex Terra Foundation with permission of RTMP; 46: O. Louis Mazzatenta/National Geographic Image Collection; 47: NHMPL ; 48: with permission of RTMP, AB; 49 (left): Hesperornis by Eleanor Kish reproduced with permission of CMN, Ottawa, Canada; 49 (right): with permission of RTMP, AB; 50-51: Annie St–Jean, reproduced with permission of CMN, Ottawa, Canada; 52: Jordan Mallon; 53 : Richard Martin, reproduced with permission of CMN, Ottawa, Canada; 54: 2002 Paul Souders/WorldFoto; 55: by Joe Tucciarone; 56: Dinosaur Provincial Park/Alberta Community Development; 57: with the permission of RTMP, AB; 58: De Agostini/NHMPL; 59 (left): courtesy Wendy Sloboda-Routley; 59 (right): CP (Jeff McIntosh); 60: by Jim Zuckerman; 61: courtesy Hans-Dieter Sues; 62: Jenny Halstead/NHMPL; 63: with permission of RTMP, AB; 64: 2002 Paul Souders/WorldFoto; 65: Marilyn Fraser © 1990; 66: NHMPL; 67: by Joe Tucciarone; 68: Robert Clark/Aurora; 70: with permission of RTMP, AB; 71: NHMPL; 72-73: with permission of the Royal Ontario Museum © ROM; 74: CP (Jeff McIntosh); 75 (top overlay): courtesy Darla Zelenitsky; 75 (top): Bruce Selyem/Museum of the Rockies; 75 (bottom): courtesy Darla Zelenitsky; 76: The Extinction of the Dinosaurs by Eleanor Kish reproduced with permission of CMN, Ottawa, Canada; 77: with permission of RTMP, AB; 79: by Jim Zuckerman; 80-81: courtesy Donna L. Sloan; 82 (left): by Donna L. Sloan with permission of RTMP, AB; 83 (top): courtesy Donna L. Sloan; 83 (bottom): with permission of the RTMP; 84-85 (main background image): with permission of the RTMP, AB; 84-85: (collage) credits can be found on original pages; 88: by Jim Zuckerman; 89: De Agostini/NHMPL.

Index